Uncle Tom's Campus

Uncle Tom's Campus

Ann Jones

PRAEGER PUBLISHERS

New York • Washington • London

The incidents and people described in this book
are drawn from life, with identifying features
changed to protect individuals, who are more
sinned against than sinning.

PRAEGER PUBLISHERS
111 Fourth Avenue, New York, N.Y. 10003, U.S.A.
5, Cromwell Place, London SW7 2JL, England

Published in the United States of America in 1973
by Praeger Publishers, Inc.

Library of Congress Catalog Card Number: 72-83005

Printed in the United States of America

For Pat, Charles, and Arto,
who know about respect

Contents

Acknowledgments

I am indebted to officers of the Bureau of Higher Education, United States Office of Education, who made files
available to me and helped me to interpret certain parts of
their contents.

Several friends have thoughtfully criticized one draft or
another of the manuscript: Mary Dalton Howard, Mary Lea
Meyersohn, Pat Lewis Sackrey, Charles Sackrey, Arto Woods,
Elizabeth Barad, and my extraordinary editor, Gladys Topkis.
Corinne Davis offered unfailing insight, and Reg Holmes
constant encouragement.

Quiet and beautiful work-places were generously provided
by other friends: Ernest Wyatt, Catherine and John Register,
Caroline Sly, and the members of The Deadly Nightshade—
Anne Bowen, Pamela Brandt, and Helen Hooke.

Finally, for the friendship of "Thomas College" students,
who prompted this book and taught me so much, I will
always be grateful.

This book is the better for having had a lot of help from
my friends; its failings, of course, are my own.

Uncle Tom's Campus

"When you buck against me, you're bucking against power, rich white folk's power, the nation's power—which means government power! . . . And I'll tell you something your sociology teachers are afraid to tell you. . . . If there weren't men like me running schools like this, there'd be no South. Nor North, either. No, and there'd be no country—not as it is today. You think about that. . . ."

—Dr. Bledsoe, President of a Negro college, in Ralph Ellison's *Invisible Man*

1

The Making of an Abolitionist

I drove toward my destination through rolling country on a highway slashed across hills of scraggly pine and scrub oak, across fields of dusty wildflowers. The landscape appeared deceptively tranquil; yet this was no country for a leisurely stroll. It was a land of sandburs hidden in the ocher grass, a land of sudden grasshoppers as dry and brittle as the parching dirt. The heat waves shimmered upward in the still air, rippling the scene so that one saw it as if through water. I drove into the outskirts of the city, past the hamburger stands, past the farm stores displaying stacked bags of fertilizer and green-webbed plastic lawn chairs, past motel row, where the orange and white pennons of a Holiday Inn drooped in the August heat, limp with the russet weight of dust—past the plastic and chromium commercial fringe worn on the hemline of every all-American city.

I came upon a faded, red-grimed sign directing me to my objective, Thomas College, the school at which I was to teach for a year. Following the direction indicated by the sign, I passed through a shabby shantytown and emerged from the city again amid farms, where a second weathered sign sent me back toward the city I had just left. After completing the round trip without finding anything resembling a college, I drove into a gas station to ask directions. I switched off the air conditioner and opened the window to a sheet of blistering dusty air as the young black attendant sidled reluctantly toward my car.

"Hello," I called. "I'm looking for Thomas College. Can you tell me how to get there?"

The young man, suddenly preoccupied with removing a grease spot from the elbow of his grimy coverall, shrugged and mumbled a barely audible "No, ma'am."

"Well, I'm sure it's around here someplace," I prompted, but the young man was transfixed, staring at the delivery slot of the ancient Dr. Pepper machine as though expecting an imminent vision. "Is there someone else around the station who might be able to tell me where the college is?" I asked.

The young man rubbed more vigorously at his elbow with an anxious thumb and shook his head. "No, ma'am," he muttered.

Tired after three days of driving and dizzy from the oppressive heat, I was frankly impatient with the attendant's muteness. "Look," I said curtly, "I want to use your telephone. Where is it?" Uncomfortable, he shifted his weight from one bare, dusty foot to the other and detached his busy thumb from his elbow long enough to gesture vaguely in the direction of the station building. Inside I found a battered telephone directory, called the city police department, and asked for directions to Thomas College.

"Well," the desk officer replied, "it's somewhere out in the west end of town."

"Yes," I said, "I know that, but I've driven all over the west end of town and can't find it. Right now I am at the corner of State and Magnolia streets. Can you direct me from here?"

"Oh, well," he drawled, "if yer out that way, jes' ask a nigger." And he slammed down the receiver. Cursing into the now silent phone, I glimpsed outside the dusty window the young attendant, still staring raptly into the entrails of the soda machine.

The following day I found the college, two blocks from the gas station where I had sought directions. A few days later, during college registration, I met the young attendant again; he was entering his third year at Thomas. My first frustrated attempt to find my new home seemed to have been an omen, a warning, an oracle unspoken by a perverse and sinister Dr. Pepper skulking in his faded green machine.

It was only by chance that I had come to teach at a black college in the South. During the previous winter, while completing my doctoral dissertation at a Midwestern university, I had begun looking about for a job teaching my specialties, modern and American literature. With several years of teaching experience behind me, I seemed assured of a good position; but getting a job was not that easy. After confidently notifying dozens of schools that I was available to accept a post, I discovered that they were not willing to interview me; few of them even condescended to answer my letters. I traveled to the annual convention of my profession, the yearly cattle market at which young Ph.D.'s on the hoof present themselves to the highest bidder. In a tight job market, however, the young men were finding the bidding low; the women were finding that no one wanted to speak with them at all. Baffled and growing bitter, I signed up with a placement bureau designed to provide teachers for smaller colleges that could not afford to do their recruiting individually.

A few months later, I had forgotten all about the placement bureau and resolved to spend my upcoming year of unemployment on a research project. Then, to my surprise,

I received a long-distance telephone call from a man who identified himself as the president of Thomas, a small black college in the South. Would I, he asked, accept a position as English professor? I inquired whether he had obtained my official transcripts and references from my university and learned that he had not. He was offering me a job on the strength of the rudimentary information I had furnished to the forgotten placement bureau. When he assured me that I would be able to teach courses in my special areas and named a salary far beyond my expectations, I accepted. But when I informed my dissertation adviser—a realistic fellow who had told me that as a woman I "would never get a decent job anyway"—of my new position and salary, he peered suspiciously over his horn-rimmed glasses and scoffed, "There must be a catch somewhere." There was. And the "catch" is the subject of this book.

I stress the accidental circumstances of my accepting this position to make it clear that I did not go south with an ax in hand to grind, that I did not go to a black college with a missionary zeal to save my brethren. I went simply to do the job for which I had been trained—one that I enjoyed. Thomas College was the only school that offered me an opportunity to teach. I anticipated being able to learn from my experience about the South and about the operation of a black college. The Southern black students in the university classes I was teaching at the time, however, warned me that I would find life in the South different and less than congenial.

"We'll be reading about you in the papers," they said when they learned that I was determined to go. "Yeah!" 'Little English professor found hanging from big tree!' "

"Now listen," I argued, "I'm not going on any crusade. The school hired me to teach, and I'm going to teach."

"Oh man!" Melvin from Louisiana cried, apparently

amazed at my ignorance. "Just 'cause they hired you to teach don't mean they really want you to teach."

"And just what is that supposed to mean?"

"You'll find out. Man, I had some friends went to that school once. Lasted about two weeks. You'll find out."

One of the first things I found out after moving to the South despite these warnings was that, as a white woman working and living in the black community, I was almost totally isolated. I was cut off from the white community, partly by their ostracism of me and partly by my own inability to relate to people whose fundamental assumptions about life differed so much from mine. Although there probably were some sympathetic white people in the community, I never met them. Similarly, I was excluded from the black community by the blacks' distrust, suspicion, and fear.

The operations of the college—which this book describes— added to my problems. Teaching at the college, I was subjected to the usual bureaucratic gobbledygook, harassment, and make-work with several ingenious flourishes that I had not encountered before. I incurred the attacks of colleagues who saw my presence as threatening, in one way or another, to their own positions. And, saddest of all, although most easily overcome, I faced the distrust of students, most of whom had never had a white teacher before.

These burdens, added to my sense of isolation, appeared acutely dangerous to me. To become totally involved in the situation, it seemed to me, would be to invite active reprisals or paranoia. Consequently, to protect my own emotional well-being, I had to detach myself as best I could and adopt the point of view of observer of my own behavior as well as that of others. This book is the product of those observations.

I must quickly add that I am not a social scientist; my training is in literature, not sociology. Lacking the tech-

niques to engage in a more systematic study of my surround-
ings, I simply gathered impressions, which slowly formed
themselves into a larger picture. Yet, even had I had the
training in sociological methodology, I would not have been
able to undertake a formalized investigation of the college;
for, although I adopted the psychological stance of observer,
I was not apart from the college but a part of it. To openly
attempt systematic study of the institution would have made
my position as a teacher untenable, and good teaching was
my first commitment.

Teaching in itself was difficult enough, for the duplicity of
the administrators, the personal and professional jealousies
of colleagues, and the distrust of students set up barriers
that had to be patiently surmounted and prompted many
rumors about what I was "really doing" at the college. Not
understanding that a white teacher (particularly a young
woman) might come to their school simply to teach, professors and students alike fabricated elaborate explanations
of my presence. Some contended that I was a white racist
who would teach "lies" in a deliberate attempt to "hold the
colored back" by misinforming them. Many members of the
college had heard vaguely of a "black revolution" and
fancied themselves part of it, although their whispered
bravado indicated only the most naive understanding of
contemporary black movements. Nevertheless, for a time it
was widely believed that I was an agent of the FBI, CIA,
Ku Klux Klan, or simply "them," sent to the college to spy
out "what the colored were planning." I confronted that
tale squarely, telling my students that if I were in fact an
agent I would do my spying where the people *had* a plan;
and the students reluctantly recognized the absurdity of the
rumor.

Then, late in the second semester, the chairman of my
department birthed a new rumor. She began to tell students
that I was writing a book about the college, a book in

which I intended to portray black people as stupid, lazy, and inferior. For a time I laughed about this new rumor, for it so obviously contained not my views on blacks but those of the chairman, who was herself black, in race if not in spirit. But as I thought through the problems of the institution as I had come to understand it, I began to feel compelled to speak about them. Perhaps, I thought, I *should* write a book. Ironically, then, it was the anxious fantasy of one of my colleagues that suggested this report.

In order to protect the privacy of individuals and of the institution, I have changed the name of the school and either altered or left deliberately vague certain identifying information. The characters I describe are composite types, imaginary individuals made up from the observed behavior of many people. They are in no way intended as actual portraits of living people. To further protect the college and its staff, I have attempted to disguise its documents when I felt it necessary to quote from them; all items presented as quotations from the college catalogue, faculty guide, HEW reports, and similar sources are not literal quotations but paraphrases, approximating the original phrasing and tone as closely as possible. My purpose has been to convey factual incidents and the spirit of the place as objectively as possible while safeguarding the privacy of the school and the real people concerned.

In reporting on the college, I have been able to draw only an incomplete and shadowy picture. Many important pieces of the puzzle are conspicuously missing. For example, I would like to have reported on the backgrounds of the administrators, trustees, and faculty who ran the college, but in most cases I found no way to elicit this information. These people are members of the black middle class, most of whom have struggled to get where they are, and some of whom apparently have arrived by rather devious paths. Aside from spinning occasional anecdotes of a public and inspirational nature, they are generally secretive about their histories. Even campus gossip—a fierce and deadly serious activity—provided little historical information, concentrating of necessity on current scandal.

I also would like to have presented more information on the backgrounds of the students: their homes and families, their reasons for coming to Thomas College, their ambitions and goals. But the students too were covert about their lives. Early in the first semester, when I asked my freshman English classes to write compositions on "Why I Came to Thomas College," I felt apologetic for the triteness of this hackneyed topic, but I could not have anticipated the students' reaction to the assignment. Most of them bristled at being asked to write on such a "personal" theme and, with their suspicions aroused, produced only one or two lines: "I came because I was supposed to," "because of many reasons of my own," " because it was here." At the end of the year, filling out an evaluation report on one of my composition courses, a girl wrote: "Now I see I can write better when I write about me and things I did in my life. I did not like to do it when I thought you only wanted to spy on Negroes."

The black students were particularly reticent toward their white teacher, but they were also reluctant to disclose themselves to one another. And since most of the students came from very poor families, they tended to glamorize their histories. I often heard students narrate entirely different and contradictory stories about their families and their own experiences on different occasions to different audiences. Many times students gave me information that I knew to be untrue, occasionally even when they must have been aware that I already knew the truth. One young man, for example, told a group of students in my presence an elaborate tale about how he had "told off" another teacher, completely undeterred by the fact that I had been present during his interview with the other teacher and knew his account to be a fabrication. Thinking that he was trying to use me as a silent witness to lend authority to his tale, I contradicted him, and he was genuinely surprised and startled that my version of the encounter differed considerably from his. I do not think that the students consciously lied very often; I believe they merely "decorated" the truth. And probably in a great many cases, their world of fantasy replaced a world of fact too bleak to bear.

One particularly wants facts and figures on what happens to the students during their stay at the college, during the process of their education. What are their aspirations as freshmen, and how do these hopes—which of course reflect a student's image of his "self"—change over the years at school? How does a student develop academically at the school? Does the tendency of his performance indicate a turning on or a turning off? Since, to my knowledge, the college has never undertaken a study of the desires and needs of its students, the only statistical clue to such questions might be the students' transcripts of grades. Such student records, however, were available only to certain trusted faculty members, and I was not among them. In fact, I did not even have access to the transcripts and files of those students who were officially my advisees. Thus, I have had to rely for information about the students' experience of the college on the word of the students themselves, although that testimony is naturally biased by the attempt of each student to present himself in the best possible light. That bias, I feel, should not disqualify the information, for in a larger sense a student's felt experience of the college, what he believes to be true, is more "true" than the empirical facts of his association with it.

One also wants facts and figures on what happens to the students after they leave college. Why do so many drop out or get expelled (about one-third of the student body each year), and what becomes of them? Where do the graduates go? What jobs do they secure? What part do they take in the life of their communities? Most colleges keep records of their graduates as a matter of course, for the subsequent careers of alumni reflect upon the quality of their school. But, Thomas College kept no such records. Once, when I was helping the dean of studies prepare an application for a federal grant, he composed a glowing paragraph about the "success" of Thomas graduates. I suggested that his point would be strengthened by including statistics on the employment of alumni, and although apparently surprised at the novelty of the idea, he acknowledged that "maybe we could find that out sometime." A survey of Thomas graduates, however, would be a major undertaking, beyond the interest of the college, and clearly beyond the scope of this study.

By far the largest missing piece of the Thomas College puzzle is statistical information about the budget. Where does the money come from, and where does it go? In answer to these questions, I have been able to give only the most general information. For reasons that I think will become clear, the college did not make such financial information publicly available. Nor is it available in any standard reference sources that I have consulted. Convinced that some of the college's money was contributed by the U.S. Department of Health, Education, and Welfare—although the college did not announce this fact—I wrote to HEW asking to examine its files on Thomas. When months had passed with no response to my inquiry, I wrote again; and this time, after only three months, I received a reply and a list of the grants awarded to Thomas during the preceding four years. Encouraged, I wrote again to an official in the Bureau of Higher Education asking for an appointment to examine the annual reports of the college filed in compliance with the Higher Education Act of 1965, the legislation under which the grants had been given.

In response to my letter, I received a frantic telephone call from a senior officer in the bureau. Why, he asked, did I want to see the records? What was I doing? How was I going to use the information? Responsible for administering federal grants to such institutions, he wanted to make sure that I would use the information "in the best interests of our colleges." He was reluctant to give me an appointment, explaining that he couldn't let "just anyone" examine the bureau's files. He feared that if he let one person into his bureau, "everyone will want to come." I assured him that I was not just anyone but rather a professor at a well-known college engaged in a legitimate education research project and that there seemed little reason to fear a massive public invasion of the files of an obscure government bureau. Nevertheless, he required a full written statement of my project before he would grant me an appointment. His major fear, and the apparent source of his paranoid fantasies, was that information in his files might be used to discredit one of "his" institutions.

"Are these files a matter of public record?" I asked him. He launched into a justification of his hesitancy, but I interrupted to repeat the question. When I had asked it a third time, I finally received an answer.

"Well, yes," he said, "they are. But we have to make sure that they will be used in the right way. After all," he said, giving the whole game away, "these colleges are our bread and butter."

So I traveled to Washington and examined the reports of Thomas College. The facts and figures gained from those reports—and some interpretations—are included in this account. They don't reveal, however, as much as they conceal, for the official report forms of the Bureau of Higher Education are noteworthy chiefly for their lack of detail. Most items called for can be answered in lumpy, imprecise figures or grandiose rhetoric. Then, too, I found the Thomas reports inconsistent. Several forms require that figures be provided for a three-year period; in the Thomas file, the 1969 report might list one set of figures for 1968, while the 1970 report might offer completely different figures for 1968. The inconsistencies had apparently passed unnoticed, however, for the bureau does not seem to compare one report to the next; the discrepancies I pointed out were a surprise to the officer in charge of the Thomas file. Fragmentary and probably inaccurate as the official Thomas figures are, I offer them nevertheless in the course of this report as the only statistical evidence I could lay hands on.

Although several of these figures may seem suspicious, I wish to make clear that I am not accusing anyone responsible for the administration of the college or its funds of dishonesty. My point is simply that the funds do not seem to be handled efficiently. Consequently, the investment of public money, in this case, seems to produce minimal positive returns while ensuring the continuation of an institution that yields, in my view, disastrous social results. Given the nature of the college, I do not see that the results can be otherwise.

One need not impute dishonest intentions or conduct to Thomas officials to explain the meager returns on the money invested. The college has undoubtedly accomplished some positive changes during the past three or four years by recruiting better qualified teachers, developing a few new courses, and expanding the physical plant. Nevertheless, the rapid turnover in faculty—particularly among the best qualified faculty—precludes long-range planning for real educational reform. A similarly high rate of turnover at certain administrative levels impedes reform of institutional life; the plan of one official is too often replaced the following year by that of another. The campus facilities remain inadequate to provide for the basic needs of the students; the greatest weakness of almost all the students is in reading, but while the lone reading teacher labors with grossly insufficient space and equipment, serving only a small portion of the student body, the college solicits $3,500 from the government to buy a phase contrast and bright field IQ microscope and another $18,000 for an EM-Elimiskop-51 for its new introductory physics course. Such topsy-turvy lists of priorities will probably continue to be produced by the college as long as the instability of the faculty and lower levels of administration inhibits intelligent planning. And that instability will probably continue as long as the college is operated on the pattern of a paternalistic plantation.

Thomas might yet be transformed into an educational institution by a massive infusion of money and—more important—a complete overhaul of its philosophy and operations by highly qualified administrators and faculty. Anything short of that—including the three-quarters of a million dollars invested in driblets during recent years by the Department of Health, Education, and Welfare—will produce only enough superficial changes to foster the illusion of progress without its substance. To justify the federal expenditures already made, and to encourage more, the college must evince some signs of advancement, but its impulse so far has been to shun real revision and reform in favor of adding a new frill here, a new furbelow there. The maxim of the college has been—as the following account will illustrate—"You won't taste the cake if the sugar frosting is thick enough." My own inclination, when the cake is moldy, is to throw it out.

That inclination, of course, represents a personal bias, and since this report is based less upon empirical evidence and more upon my experience of the college, I should make my bias clear at the outset. In any circumstances, I take the side of those who seem to me to be oppressed, not through sympathy for the underdogs, but through identification with them. As a woman in academia, I have long felt the operation of prejudice, economically and professionally. As student, woman, wife, I have experienced the sense of helplessness, frustration, and, ultimately, rage that attends the feeling that "others" have significant control over one's life. Growing up female has given me an all too intimate knowledge of that psychological manipulation that produces stereotypical behavior. And as one of very few whites to live in a particular Southern black community, I have experienced racial prejudice in a way not usually open to white Americans: as the *object* of that prejudice. Thus, I must acknowledge in this case a strong predisposition to side with the students, whom I saw as oppressed, and to reject the arguments other teachers and administrators used to rationalize their positions.

Although this account depicts a black college, its main concern is not race but the dynamics of oppression as they occur in a particular institution. I do not mean to suggest that Thomas College is typical of black institutions, for among black colleges and universities, as among their white counterparts, there are the sound and the unsound, the excellent and the inferior. Many incidents recounted in this report will find echoes in the experience of anyone familiar with American academic life. At almost any college, black or white, registration is likely to be chaotic, health services are apt to be inadequate, official meetings may be routinely tedious, and the food will probably confirm the notorious reputation of institutional cafeterias everywhere. Many of the conclusions of this report apply to *all* students, regardless of color, at every level of education, for our schools in America clearly are less a means of education than a means of socialization and technocratic manpower training. They are a means of producing "normal" and, in R. D. Laing's phrase, "absurd people." The fact that this account concerns a black college adds complexity to the general problem, for here is not just another case of educationist bureaucrats oppressing students but a case of black educators unwittingly oppressing black students at the service of a white society. That the black educators described perform this task so well is, of course, the result of their own socialization into an oppressive and racist society.

I wish to stress this point here because in the record that follows I often seem unduly harsh in my portrayal of the black educators. If certain figures appear to be villains, it is because that is the only side of most of my collegaues I knew well enough to describe. I experienced them in their official capacities as functionaries within the institution, and insofar as this account is a functional analysis of that institution, they must appear as villains. A man ceases to seem a villain when one perceives his humanity—his sufferings, doubts, frustrations, insecurity, love, hopes, aspirations—but the people from whom my characters are composed found it necessary to conceal their humanity in order to perform their public function. Covertness became a way of life. And, unfortunately, most of them, in one way or another, considered me a threat; I have no doubt that they were even more defensive toward me than they were toward one another.

The black characters who appear to be the villains of this piece have become what they seem to be under the pressure of a racist society. And, as a white person, I have conspired unwittingly and unwillingly in making them what they are. Like the New England–reared wife of the Southern slave owner who beat her slave to death because she "could not bear to see his suffering," I believe that the severity of my own attack upon the black educators stems in part from my inability to bear what my own race has done to them. In an important sense, it is these "villains" who are the real tragic figures of the record that follows.

2

The New Slavery

Thomas College looks like a run-down reformatory. When I first saw it, I was amazed that the county or the state had built a prison complex in the midst of the community; but a wooden signboard, its red paint sun-bleached to a dull pink, announced that this complex *was* the college. The campus stretched for several blocks behind a rusty chain-link fence. The grass, withered by the heat, was covered with a sifting of fine red dust. Despite a scattering of shade trees, the campus appeared barren and desolate. It was not so much the unrelieved flatness of the land and the sparseness of the vegetation that gave the place its atmosphere of bleakness. It was the buildings.

Flanking the main road were some new dormitories, wide-windowed, glass-doored, nondescript modern structures that might have been small hospitals or office buildings. They were the largest buildings on the campus and the first to be seen, but they seemed to fade away from the eye; one passed without noticing them and saw instead the other campus buildings, more distinctive if no less ugly. There were one-story buildings hugging the ground, two-story cubes, and a few three-story hulks dominating the campus. All were the same faded red brick, and, except for one, to which a pillared portico had been added as an afterthought, none was distinguished by the least bit of architectural detail. Some were office buildings, two or three were classroom buildings, and several were domitories, but it was impossible to determine anything about their respective functions from their outward appearance. A child might have built the college from the prefabricated pieces of a construction set.

On the basis of their appearance, it was equally impossible to tell the age of the buildings. Many of them had been built in the thirties and forties; several others in the teens. In the sixties, when federal funds became available, the college had started building again; a cafeteria and an administration building, like the two modern dormitories, were recent additions but had been built to conform to the established architecture of the campus, so that it was difficult to tell which building was fifty years old and which five. All were fashioned in the same ageless institutional "style," with no grace or charm, no distinction or relief; and all were in obvious need of repair.

The whole scene was flat, lacking perspective, like a picture crudely painted on a canvas backdrop for a senior class play. But in that flatness, one detail stood out: almost all the windows were covered with heavy steel bars. The bars were supposed to prevent the theft of records from the offices, books from the library, machines from the business center. In recent years, I was told later, buildings had been ransacked and valuable equipment stolen. But the bars were built into the brick structures; they were not a recent addition. They suggested that the college had been the victim, not of occasional vandals or burglars, but of continual and systematic looting. Even the faculty was not above suspicion, for it was the policy of the college that all equipment must be requisitioned by, and assigned to, specific faculty members, who had to account for it at the end of the term or have the replacement cost deducted from their salary. It was never clear who the culprits were—local citizens, students, faculty, or the college administrators themselves. But it was immediately apparent that the college was on the defensive. It was the bars, more than anything else, that gave the place the atmosphere of a prison—or a fortress—keeping outsiders out and, safely locked within its own walls, its own secrets.

The college is located in a small city, on the outer fringes of the black side of town, shielded from the white world by a rambling residential area. The houses in the black section, mostly small frame bungalows, reflect the financial circumstances of their owners; many are neat and trim, freshly painted, with lawns, even when parched and dry, still raked and orderly. Others show peeling paint, broken windows, sagging roofs, all the afflictions of old houses when there is no money to maintain them. Some are mere shanties, leaning precariously on the brick stilts that serve in place of proper foundations. But all these grades of houses can be found on every street, a tumbling shanty next door to an eminently respectable, newly painted bungalow. There is no sense of an economic neighborhood but rather of the precarious position of each individual. You get a house where and when you can get it. You may later have the money to add a patio, complete with decorative wrought iron grillwork, to your shanty, or you may lose your job or your husband and sit helplessly by while the roof caves in and the paint peels off your once fine little home. You can't do much planning ahead.

Only on a couple of streets is there any evidence of a neighborhood composed of members of the same economic class; these are the upper-middle-class streets that could appear in any white suburb. The brick ranch homes, the two-car garages, the barbecue pits, the well-dressed children riding their shiny new bicycles or romping with the family poodle—all are straight out of the pages of *Better Homes & Gardens*. Yet even on these streets, something may give it all away. In the middle of a block of impressive ranch homes is one that has never been completed. The brick facing has not been applied; the windows are gaping holes; the yard is knee-deep in weeds. Someone, who thought he was on the way up, didn't make it. In the new white neighborhoods, the housing developer takes care of such problems; he builds the neighborhood, then sells the houses to people who can make the payments. But no developer would be fool enough to build an upper-middle-class neighborhood for blacks; he could never be assured of selling his houses. So in the black community it is every man for himself. Your new $25,000 house may wind up next door to a deserted ruin, but that— if you are black—is the chance you take. Some of the upper-middle-class blacks have built their beautiful homes in the midst of the shanties and bungalows. Their yards are bigger, invariably fenced, and their dogs are bigger—Shepherds and Dobermans, just in case their less fortunate neighbors should be tempted—but there they are.

In the midst of the black community, toward the western edge of it, is the college. Perhaps it is only coincidence that most of the middle-class homes are on one side of the campus and the motley lower classes on the other side, with the college in between. But its location indicates the transitional role that most of its students expect or hope it will play in their lives. Most of them come from the shanties; whether those shanties are in Georgia, Mississippi, Louisiana, Tennessee, or Florida makes little difference. And most of them aspire to the middle-class street. They want the brick ranch home, and they would like the neighborhood that should go with it, but if it must be in the middle of shantytown, that's all right; at least the neighbors will know that they have "made it."

Perhaps those aspirations could be turned to advantage by the college, used as motivation and incentive to encourage the students to excel at their studies. Perhaps—but it doesn't work that way. For there are other, more important factors than education underlying the housing patterns in this black community.

It doesn't take the students long to discover that the occupants of the brick ranch houses are not necessarily the best-educated members of the black community. Some of the graduates of the college work in the maintenance department of the school, others are waiters at downtown hotels or eastside country clubs; they live in modest homes on the wrong side of the college. In the ranch homes live the bootleggers, the undertakers, the self-ordained ministers, and those "businessmen" whose specific business no one knows. The black doctors and dentists, for all their college degrees, cannot afford the homes that the black preachers, uneducated but "called" to the ministry, occupy.

The pattern of the community is reproduced on the college campus itself. At one end of the campus stand the faculty houses, a scattering of once white bungalows in a barren field. The paint peels; the roofs sag and dip; some houses lean so far off their original foundations that the doors and windows no longer close. In these dilapidated shacks live some of the most important members of the faculty, among them the first black Ph.D. on the staff, an ancient lady whose years of study and struggle have earned her the right to live in a shanty much like the one in which she was born. Her constant preaching to the students about the value of an education makes little impression on kids who recognize a shack when they see one. At the other end of the campus stands the president's home. The imposing brick house with the formal colonnade is provided by the college, but everybody knows that the president himself owns another home just as fine in the neighborhood. Inside the official residence, where some students are employed as servants, is the white-carpeted, sunken living room, tastefully furnished by an interior decorator in off-white, silk-covered furniture. Occasionally student leaders are invited to the home for refreshments served on fine bone china; the silver candelabra help to create the atmosphere of elegance, lending a soft glow to the creamy white walls. The student leaders, like the faculty members who on rare occasions are also invited for refreshments, know that an invitation from the president is a command, a summons from the master.

Each fall the faculty and staff are summoned to the big house for the annual faculty reception. As ordered, they gather to pay respect to President Greeson, courtly and reserved within the white walls of his fortress, with the aristocratic Mrs. Greeson, professor of business, by his side. Here, over coffee and cake, the faculty falls into its natural groups, each professor seeking out those with whom he feels affinity. The *grandes dames,* Dr. Harder and Mrs. Hood, arch-rivals and contending gurus of the faculty, are installed in adjacent silken armchairs like suspicious chaperones at the prom. The exiles—a Cuban, an Arab, an Indonesian, a Jamaican, and a German—whose strange wanderings have finally carried them to Thomas, cling to corners, darting out like quick birds to shake a hand, exchange a broken-English pleasantry, searching for a friend, grateful for an acquaintance. Filling the center of the room stand the palace guard, the inner core of the faculty and staff, those who have "been around" for a few years, many as students before joining the faculty. Resplendent now in cocktail gowns and dark suits, they take the occasion with deadpan seriousness, masking behind cool dark faces the complacent grins of the elect. Apart from all these lounges Mr. Rogers, the young white chairman of the education department, the princeling, the right hand of President Greeson, and the most articulate and effective teacher and committeeman on the faculty. Here he plays a calm, reflective role, balancing a cake plate upon a creased knee and smiling wryly at the clowning of his white buddy from the history department, Mr. Willingham, the campus fat boy and self-appointed buffoon. Then, the reception hour over, the faculty and staff, having looked each other over, depart on cue, leaving the soiled china to the student dishwashers and the splendid white room to President Greeson.

There are other impressive homes in the black community besides President Greeson's, and many of them belong to people connected with the college. One of the most imposing is owned by a former college officer who has become involved in "business" and gained a fine reputation among local whites as the "political leader" of the black community; given enough incentive, he is able to deliver the black vote to the most conservative candidates. But the man most highly regarded in the black community as a symbol of "making it," the vice-president in charge of business management, has been with the college longer than any other administrator. To most members of the community he is "Mr. College." Among the students he is famous for being the only black man in town with a brick doghouse. The legend of the brick doghouse is often repeated derisively by students who have been around for a few years and know that the man's income seems to exceed any reasonable expectations for someone in his position; but if one has grown up in a broken-down shanty, that derision cannot conceal a good deal of envy. And everyone knows that Mr. College is not a member of the faculty; in fact, he may not even have the "benefit" of a college education. Still, he is the most successful man on campus.

On the college campus, then, there are at least two value systems operating. The obvious lesson of modern capitalism to be learned from the housing patterns, on and off campus, is that the man closest to the cash register can do the best. Although that economic principle is clear, it is overlaid with the vestiges of a bygone social system, a system under which the master rules from his big house and the slaves, down in the quarters, do his bidding. On the college campus, the physical pattern—the faculty in the slave quarters, the students and staff in the outbuildings, the president on his cool veranda—is only the outward sign of a pervasive plantation psychology. It is this plantation psychology that determines the institutional character of the school.

In performing the highly specialized task for which it was created, Thomas College—and others like it—functions as what sociologists call a "total institution" or "closed system." Such institutions—whether they be prisons, concentration camps, religious houses, mental asylums, or boarding schools—are characterized by several distinctive social arrangements. Sociologist Erving Goffman provides a succinct description:

> First, all aspects of life are conducted in the same place and under the same single authority. Second, each phase of the member's daily activity is carried on in the immediate company of a large batch of others, all of whom are treated alike and required to do the same things together. Third, all phases of the day's activities are tightly scheduled, with one activity leading at a prearranged time into the next, the whole sequence of activities being imposed from above by a system of explicit formal rulings and a body of officials. Finally, the various enforced activities are brought together into a single rational plan purportedly designed to fulfill the official aims of the institution.[1]

All of these characteristics prevail at Thomas. Because very few of the 500 enrolled students live at home or off campus, almost all of them work, play, eat, and sleep "on the yard." The student's daily class schedule, dictated by his adviser, is fitted into time slots between his required atten-

[1] Erving Goffman, *Asylums: Essays on the Social Situation of Mental Patients and Other Inmates* (New York: Doubleday, 1961), p. 6.

dance at meals, chapel periods, and curfews. He is brought
to this regimented and encompassing institution to be shaped
by its Christian atmosphere and to be given "preparation
for life."

Most of the Thomas faculty and staff return to their
homes at the end of the school day, spending the evening
in the company of family and friends. Since most of them
live within a few blocks of the campus, however, and since
life at the college provides a favorite topic of off-hour conversation, they are never very far removed from the institution. Some faculty members are even more confined; they
live, as I did, in the college-owned shanties on the campus.
And, as noted, the clearest representative of authority within
the institution, its president, lives in the "big house" on the
campus, making his presence felt at all times. Most faculty
and staff members are freer to come and go than the students, yet they, too, are essentially inmates of the institution.

Thomas College differs from such institutions as concentration camps, prisons, and slaveholding plantations in at
least one important respect: its inmates are not physically
confined within its walls. Presumably students and staff are
present on the campus voluntarily; they have not been committed or sentenced. Since the world outside is readily available to its inmates, the college might be expected to exert
only limited influence over them. The member of any residential college may also be a worker in the off-campus
world, a member of an off-campus social or civic group, a
member of a family; his role as teacher or student is only
one of many complementary roles in his life. At Thomas,
however, life outside the campus tends to reinforce the patterns of the institution, for the off-campus society is segregated. Black women who go to the central business area to
shop may find that trying on clothes is a privilege reserved
for whites only. Young black men who take jobs in the local

factories may be directed to use the "colored" washroom. White churches, clubs, and civic organizations are closed to blacks. The only off-campus places where a black student or faculty member can feel comfortable are the black club, patronized by other campus people, or the black churches, which preach the college's doctrine of piety and humility. The black college member who ventures into the outside world learns only what the college is already teaching him: that he is an inferior being.

The city that constitutes the world beyond the walls for Thomas students originated as an agricultural center, a market town for the outlying farms. In the 1940's, with the discovery of mineral resources in the area, the town enjoyed a boom, and since that time it has tried mightily to transform itself into a center of industry. Unfortunately, the city holds few attractions for major industries: an inconvenient location, poor transportation, no pool of skilled labor, an undistinguished school system, little civic or cultural activity, and an upright citizenry that consistently votes to ban the sale of alcoholic beverages within the county. Only a few relatively small industries have been attracted to the town, importing a few managers from larger cities but recruiting as laborers the former farm workers from the area. The growth that the city has enjoyed during its period of industrialization, then, has brought no influx of a managerial class, of new citizens with different backgrounds and ideas. Instead it has brought the neighboring farmers to town, making the city increasingly parochial and insular in its attitudes and ideas.

According to the chamber of commerce, the city officially is devoted to Progress above all else. In the name of Progress, the tranquil, tree-shaded town square has been demolished to be replaced by a treeless concrete "plaza" surrounded by once picturesque old buildings newly faced with brilliant pink aluminum sheathing. From its past, the city retains only a crumbling Civil War monument, with an inscription celebrating the loyalty of local blacks, and a virulent racism that betrays the poor-white origins of most of its citizens.

The whites who today constitute about four-fifths of the city's population apparently see the blacks only as a race to be exploited and used. They build new high schools in the white neighborhoods, naming them after heroes of the Confederacy, and provide school buses for white students from outlying suburbs, including those who live within walking distance of the black high school; but they organize massive resistance to busing black children to achieve racial balance in the schools. The local school system, consequently, remains almost totally segregated. Business people commonly address blacks, no matter what academic or professional titles they may have earned in addition to the usual courtesy title, by their first names, or use the even more offensive "boy." Legitimate businesses often refuse to extend credit to blacks, while public utilities charge blacks higher deposit rates than whites. At the same time, postal addresses known to be within the black section of town are flooded with enticing brochures from loan sharks and purveyors of "special offers" of merchandise. The city has neglected to pave the dusty red streets of the black section, although its residents have paid many times over in taxes and special assessments for the curbs, gutters, and paving they should have. Only those streets in the black community that whites need to travel from one edge of the city to the other have been paved; and most white citizens, to whom the black section is an invisible area out of which their maids and janitors miraculously emerge daily, probably do not even know that the dusty shanty roads exist within the city limits. Nor do they know that the garbage service they pay for and receive is also paid for—but only rarely received—by blacks. The black community, with its red dust, its trash piles, its dilapidated schools, remains invisible.

Meanwhile the city grandiosely advertises itself as a "center of culture." Aside from a small local orchestra, however, in which blacks are not allowed to perform, the city has *no* cultural events or activities. There is an annual flower and fruit parade, complete with beauty queens in ante-bellum costumes, but that is not so much a cultural event as an economic one, for the city profits greatly from the sale of flowers and fruit grown in the area. The chief "cultural" events during the year I lived in the city were two highly publicized speeches, one by a member of the *Pueblo* crew who convinced a highly sympathetic audience that the United States should have "gone into Korea and taken back" its ill-fated spy ship, the other by a black woman who "proved" that Dr. Martin Luther King, Jr. was a Communist. Another local event that might have been significant for the black community was instead an abject failure. The special showing of a documentary film on the life of Dr. King, for the benefit of the Southern Christian Leadership Conference, was attended by only a scattering of people, none of them leaders of the black community, for it had been preceded by a massive advertising campaign conducted by the White Citizen's Council denouncing King and those who would attend the film as Communists. The city's chief source of pride and culture, however, was the drill team of baton twirlers from the local white college, a group of satin-breasted, white-booted young ladies who annually performed among fireworks facsimiles of the American flag and the screaming arrow-clawed eagle at football half time shows.

The city effectively perpetuated the old white racist attitudes and insulated itself from new ideas. The local media were all under the control of one man, whose special crusade was to have the astronauts broadcast more prayers from outer space. His television station selected from the network schedules only the most innocuous of programs—none with black actors or concern for black subjects. To fill its responsibility to broadcast a certain quota of public-service announcements it displayed between programs flashcards inscribed with one or another of the Ten Commandments. The newspaper printed no news of the black community, but—in what seemed to be a major concession—it had recently begun to print not only the names but the photographs of blacks killed in Vietnam. The news blackout—or whitewash—pertained not only to blacks but also to the young and particularly to those who opposed the war in Southeast Asia. In an unusual front-page editorial, the paper proclaimed that it would not print news of antiwar Moratorium Day demonstrations; it justified its policy by announcing that such protests "make us sick." "It is true," the editor acknowledged, "that 'the news comes first,' but a newspaper's free country comes even before that."

That was the city. And periodically the city brought its lessons to the college through white police officers. Any illegal act by a black could provide an excuse for the police to search the college dormitories, with the tacit approval of college authorities. Occasionally, they searched without an excuse, saying that they were looking for marijuana, which only a handful of the students used. Significantly, such unannounced drug raids were never carried out at the white college on the other side of town, where drug use was reportedly much more common. Sometimes the police were just angry; after a policeman had been wounded by a black man, the police continued their search of the college and the black neighborhood all night, many hours after everyone knew that the suspect had been arrested. But the lesson of racial inferiority sometimes was brought home by less disciplined hands. Carloads of drunken whites, out to "git a nigger," cruised through black neighborhoods at night, taking pot shots at pedestrians and residents who happened to be sitting on their porches. Although they have wounded several blacks, some fatally, the police are never able to apprehend them.

Intimidated by both the red-necks and the police, the inmates of Thomas College quickly learn that they are safer within the walls. The institution, then, becomes a haven from the threatening outside world. There, a student or teacher knows what is expected of him, what the rules are. There, he may be harassed and humiliated, but he will not be beaten or killed by hateful whites. Confinement to the institution, although voluntary, then becomes total.

Although, as an institution, Thomas approximates both physically and psychologically the patterns of the much older institution of slavery, the college receives almost unanimous support from all segments of society. Lower-class blacks grudgingly respect the college, envy its students, and hope that, although it has not improved their lot, it may offer opportunity to their children. To the black middle and upper classes, the college is something to be proud of, a center of higher education for members of their race. The students at the college are grateful for the "opportunity" it offers them, for in most cases their life on campus is physically more comfortable than their life at home. Paradoxically, even those students who complain most about conditions and courses at the school would be—in a showdown—its defenders, for inside the iron gates of Thomas, they are safe from the threats and intimidation of the white society.

But, if Thomas had the support of blacks alone, it would be unable to carry on. Blacks usually have little money to donate to colleges. It is the white world that keeps Thomas in business. In training blacks to be humbly accepting of their second-class status, Thomas most clearly serves the purposes of white racists who contribute to its support. But the bulk of Thomas's financial aid comes from governmental programs passed and administered by white liberals. Through educational programs of the Department of Health, Education, and Welfare, and through large grants from educational foundations, the conscience-stricken liberal purges his guilt. Having taken to heart the repeated findings of investigating commissions that America is plagued by white racism, the liberal demonstrates his "right-mindedness" by sending more money to *all* the black colleges, without bothering to ascertain the differences among them. The white racist, resigned to the high cost of segregation, endorses the check, knowing that schools like Thomas can "keep the niggers in their place." Cutting off public support to Thomas is equally unthinkable to the racist who wants to keep blacks in their own schools and to the liberal who wants to help blacks to get ahead. There is only one group of people who dislike schools like Thomas: the textbook salesmen, who know that such colleges seldom buy new books.

Thomas doesn't really need new books to carry out its archaic educational program. Its courses are based upon outmoded notions of classical education; its curricula remain largely irrelevant to the real needs and opportunities of its students. Its conservative philosophy arises from the popular, but scarcely credible, myth that, if pious black people will only educate themselves, whites will accept them and racism will miraculously disappear; yet its practices seem to be dictated by the tacit assumption that black people can never assume an equal position in American society. This paradoxical position of Thomas today has its roots in the great debate about black education, the famous controversy between Booker T. Washington and W. E. B. DuBois.

In the last decade of the nineteenth century, Washington rose to prominence as a black leader by advocating a program of vocational education. Washington argued that the races could remain separate socially while still working together for mutual progress; but to work for that progress, blacks had to be trained to take their place in the economy. Washington's program of "industrial education" attracted the support of Northern capitalist philanthropists, who saw it as a manpower training program for the industrializing South, and of Southern racists, who hoped that it would forestall the growth of a well-educated Negro leadership. Many relieved whites saw in the black's desire for industrial education his admission that manual labor was his only capability, his acceptance of permanent second-class citizenship. Despite this white support—or because of it—the industrial education movement never did achieve the goal of training black industrial workers, for it taught domestic science, agriculture, and traditional handicrafts rather than the new skills needed in a mechanized age. Industrial work in Southern mills and factories was reserved for the lower classes of whites. Black graduates of the industrial schools, if they did not become menial workers, became teachers in the black school system or, with further professional education, the doctors, lawyers, and businessmen of the black communities.

W. E. B. DuBois, the eminent sociologist from Atlanta University, on the other hand, supported vocational training —but only as *one* kind of education among others that should be open to blacks. Recognizing that educating a man was different from training a money-maker, DuBois called for liberal academic education for the teachers and leaders of the race. His concern was for the "talented tenth," the exceptional people who would "save" the race by guiding the masses toward their own betterment.

The debate between the followers of DuBois and Washington raged for at least two decades. In one Southern state a group of black leaders petitioned the state legislature in the 1880's to provide industrial education at a state normal school for blacks. But only a few years later, the state Association for Negro Teachers passed a resolution condemning strictly industrial education that forced blacks into "lower" occupations exclusively. In resolving this issue, the whites, not the blacks, had power. And few whites were willing to educate the talented tenth, or even to admit that it existed. So unpopular were DuBois's views that many white philanthropists withdrew their support from Atlanta University, forcing DuBois to resign his professorship to save the university further embarrassment. On the other hand, industrial education purported to train the muscles, not the mind. Wittingly or not, it coincided with the white man's image of the black man as a brawny, subhuman creature, as—in Eldridge Cleaver's term—the "supermasculine menial." Eventually, any black school that even pretended to offer industrial education could count on the financial support of white philanthropists. As sociologist E. Franklin Frazier has pointed out, industrial education became a "racket." [2] Booker T. Washington apparently had won the day, but even as the debate went on, other private black colleges, including Thomas, were being formed. On the development of some of these colleges, DuBois's views had a profound influence.

The major task of these colleges was the training of teachers for the black public school system. This assignment fell to the black colleges by default since white citizens would not provide adequate teacher training for blacks. From the outset the private black colleges suffered serious handicaps, of which probably the largest was the lack of money. The colleges could charge only minimal tuition fees, if any, since their students were poor. Lacking state support, such schools sought financial aid from religious denominations and philanthropies—in direct competition with one another. Until very recently, when federal aid in large doses became available to these schools, their financial health, at best, was precarious.

An obstacle more difficult for black colleges to surmount has been the poor quality of the black public school system. Throughout their history, the colleges have been overburdened with remedial work. In order to recruit a student

[2] E. Franklin Frazier, *Black Bourgeoisie: The Rise of a New Middle Class in the United States* (New York: Macmillan, 1962), p. 63.

body, many of them have had to accept graduates of un-accredited high schools and "special students" who have not graduated from high school at all. And even those students who were high school graduates usually were not prepared for true college-level studies by what the black public school system had been able to teach them. In the early years of the black colleges, finding enough students who had at least some high school training was almost impossible. The colleges themselves, consequently, were forced to establish their own elementary and secondary branches to prepare future college students. At least until the 1930's, Thomas enrolled more elementary and high school pupils than college students. In addition to operating elementary and secondary branches on its campus, Thomas also had to fragment its collegiate program into lower and upper divisions. Although the college offered a four-year program, the state Department of Education would grant it accreditation only as a two-year college. This state accreditation policy encouraged most students to leave college after two years of teacher training, inhibiting both the development of the college as a four-year institution and the development of a thoroughly trained teaching staff for the black public school system.

Despite all these handicaps, many of the newly formed black colleges tacitly rejected industrial education, choosing instead the more difficult task of providing "cultural" education. Receiving no state support, they opted for a form of higher education different from that of the state industrial schools for blacks. Following DuBois, they sought to educate the talented tenth, emulating as far as possible the liberal arts curricula of the best white colleges. Like many imitators, however, they sometimes carried their mimicry to extremes; in trying to follow the pattern of Harvard and Yale, the black colleges sometimes lost sight of the real needs of their students. And in trying to provide a largely

cultural education, they apparently proceeded on the unlikely assumption that all of their students were, in fact,
members of the talented tenth. For a long time, many of the
black denominational colleges, consequently, offered more
courses in Greek and Latin than in English.

Schools like Thomas, however, were ill equipped to present a broad classical education. Their precarious financial
situation limited the size of faculty and precluded the hiring
of specialists in each of the areas of study offered. Since
higher education for blacks previously had been all but nonexistent, Thomas in its early years probably could not have
found enough qualified black scholars for its faculty in any
case. Yet Thomas insisted upon cultural education, making
extraordinary demands on the versatility of its small faculty.
During the 1920's Thomas had only eight faculty members
at the college level. One of them held a master's degree, six
held bachelor's degrees (one from Thomas itself), and one
had no college degree at all. The small size and rudimentary
training of its faculty, however, did not deter cultural education at Thomas. The professor of English also taught Latin
courses. The professor of foreign languages also taught history, science, and philosophy. The instructor in education—
the lowest-ranking faculty member and presumably the one
who had no college degree—offered courses in educational
administration, educational psychology, anatomy, and geog-
raphy. Such versatility is sometimes expected of grade school
teachers, but it is rare in college. Obviously, few teachers
can spread themselves so thin unless instruction is being carried on at a very elementary level.

Throughout most of its history, however, Thomas has
pursued its program of cultural education with zeal, offering
little or no vocational preparation other than teacher training. Most of its students have taken the two-year teacher-
training program and gone on to teach in the Negro public
schools of the state. Few have remained to graduate from

the senior college, for despite their degrees and their knowledge of Greek and Latin, there would have been little for them to do in the segregated South—or anyplace else in the country, for that matter—except teach in black colleges.

In the 1930's, Thomas named a new and dynamic president who knew how to manipulate the educational establishment; he soon obtained full accreditation for the college, from both the state and the regional accrediting agencies, and gained financial aid from the United Negro College Fund. Later, however, the balloon burst; Thomas lost its accreditation and, in consequence, its United Negro College Fund support. Precisely when and why accreditation was withdrawn is a closely kept secret, and since the college conveniently neglects to mention its loss in the school catalogue, it has continued for years to attract students who enroll under the impression that Thomas is an accredited college.

Today, Thomas continues to be primarily a teacher-training college. Most of its graduates receive degrees in education and go out to teach in predominantly black schools in the South. Although in the training of teachers the college seems to recognize the practical need of its students to find jobs after graduation, vestiges of cultural education cling to the curricula. The official objectives of the School of Arts and Letters, as stated in the college catalogue, clearly represent the old line:

> Arts and letters are devoted to those studies which are essential in the growth of a well-rounded and cultured human being. . . . The works of such men as Aristotle, Da Vinci, Shakespeare, Bach, and Balzac have endured, and they are significant today. The soul of a liberal undergraduate education is formed from them, and, therefore, they provide a humanistic basis not only for students planning to study in graduate school but also for those contemplating a career in business or the professions.

Every student is still required to include in his curriculum from six to twelve hours of a foreign language, although French and Spanish have replaced Greek and Latin as cultural coin. Every student is still required to take at least one course in aesthetics, art, or music. And every student is required to take a strange hybrid produced by the marriage of cultural and practical education: a course officially listed in the catalogue as "Philosophy" but known popularly as Personal Hygiene, or Home Economics 1. Some departments, such as business, have been added to the college, perhaps as a concession to the advocates of vocational education, perhaps in recognition of the fact that Harvard, too, teaches business. The departments of business and home economics, however, which one might expect to be vocationally oriented, are so only in a limited way; both are primarily adjuncts to the education department, training students to be high school teachers of typing and sewing, respectively. The business student cannot become a specialist in insurance or real estate or banking; the home economics student cannot study merchandising, design, or nutrition.

Unfortunately, this problem of limited vocational choice is not confined to Thomas. For years the better black colleges have stressed the need for highly developed placement and counseling services, diversified curriculum offerings, and career information; but a 1964 study showed little change from previous studies of the vocational choices of students at black colleges. Researchers concluded that "the choices students *are* making seem to indicate that too few of these students are yet aware of choices they *could* make." [3] At Thomas, however, the college itself seems unaware of the fact that vocations formerly closed to blacks are now open. Even if they want to do so, Thomas students cannot prepare

[3] Patricia Gurin and Daniel Katz, *Motivation and Aspiration in the Negro College* (Ann Arbor, Michigan: Survey Research Center, Institute for Social Research, 1966), pp. 61, 62, 69.

for careers as psychologists, physicists, social workers, market analysts, art historians, or computer scientists. They can prepare for little except teaching.

Officially, the college offers degrees in business, home economics, biology, chemistry, math, English, social studies, music, and physical education, but most students combine one of these majors with education courses in order to have a marketable degree. The student who does not major in education may have little to show for his four years of college work. If he is interested in science, he can major in biology or chemistry, but not in physics. He can take no courses in engineering or computer science. The science departments profess to offer preprofessional training in medicine, dentistry, and nursing; but they fail to advise their students that such work could be completed more quickly and effectively at state schools that offer true preprofessional curricula. The student who is interested in the social sciences can earn a degree in social studies, a discipline comprised of little bits of history, political science, government, and economics; but he cannot major in any of those specific fields or take courses in other significant social sciences such as psychology, sociology, anthropology, or social work.

Even the student who majors in the college's strong suit —education—may find his diploma worthless. Since the college is unaccredited, its education graduates are not automatically granted certification as teachers by the state education agency. Instead, the agency must examine the graduates individually to determine whether they are, in fact, qualified for certification. Some Thomas graduates don't pass the test.

The lack of true preprofessional and professional courses at Thomas reflects more than just the residual influence of cultural education. It reflects some fundamental and pernicious assumptions by administrators about the appropriateness for blacks of certain jobs. The student who wants to become a businessman may major in business administration, but his curriculum will offer him only a semester course in business management while requiring him to take three semesters of typing and four semesters of shorthand and dictation. His degree will prepare him neither for business nor for graduate studies in business—but he will make a passable secretary.

The college currently provides two courses of study that are strictly vocational in nature, designed for those few students who are not among the talented tenth. One is a two-year course in secretarial skills offered by the secretarial science department. The other is a four-year curriculum offered by the home economics department in Vocational Nursing and Home Economics Management, designed to prepare for "positions in hospitals and homes." In other words, after four years of study in this program, the graduate may become a practical nurse or a housemaid.

The official objective of Thomas College is to use "knowledge," "truth," and "wisdom" to establish a "Christian environment" and ensure "proper maturation of the mind, body, and spirit of the developing individual." In this Christian environment, the college says, it seeks to give its students "preparation for life." The life for which it seeks to prepare them, however, is the clearly restricted life of Southern segregated society, a society in which black people are still widely supposed to be an inferior breed.

Trading on the aspirations of poor youngsters and their families, and safely hidden from outside scrutiny, the college flourishes. As an educational institution it is inefficient, ineffective, and obsolete. But as a "total institution" designed to preserve existent social arrangements, it is nearly perfect. Its value and its rationale lie in its ability to carry out effectively a program of "Negro education" dictated by a white racist society more than a century ago.

3

Down the River

To ensure its continuing smooth operation, a closed system —whether it be a slaveholding plantation or a Thomas College—must make a first impression on newcomers that is bold and lasting. Thomas could count, more or less, upon its old retainers to submit to the yoke, but, for the safety of the institution, it had to teach novices as quickly as possible the lesson of subservience. For this purpose, Thomas had devised a series of elaborate initiation rites, aimed particularly at the potentially disruptive incoming teachers and students and designed to replace their identity as free people with the obedient character of the humble slave. Like the slaves transported in chains from their native Africa, Thomas students and faculty suffered, symbolically at least, the rigors of the Middle Passage.

Even before the new students arrived for their orientation, the teachers and staff—both old and new—were put through a three-day faculty conference. During the conference, the president used one of his most effective tools—the large-group meeting—to reduce his employees to physical exhaustion and mental capitulation. The faithful faculty retainers

were given enough public recognition to revitalize their
loyalty; the new faculty—like the new students a few days
later—were given a glimpse of an ongoing institution that
had functioned perfectly well without them in the past and
could do so happily in the future. The meaningless rhetoric
and useless procedures that constituted the life of the institution seemed at first irrational and absurd; but after three
days of constant indoctrination, one began to perceive the
institution as somehow more "real" than the outside world.
The institution had a logic of its own; to accept that logic
as real and rational was to become an inmate. Fostering that
acceptance was the purpose of the faculty conference.

Those meetings constituted my introduction to Thomas
College. I approached them with the expectation that, like
faculty orientation sessions at colleges everywhere, they
would be dull but informative. My expectation, however,
soon was replaced by confusion and intimidation. Those
feelings, of course, were precisely what the conference had
been designed to elicit. Perhaps this function of the orientation sessions can best be conveyed by an account of my own
naive responses.

On the first day, a cluster of cars indicated the building
where the meetings were to be held. At the door, I was
met by a petite, middle-aged, black woman.

"Good morning," she said in a high-pitched voice, articu-
lating each word precisely. She screwed her lips into a wide
smile, but her forehead was deeply wrinkled with frowns
and her eyes were hard.

"May I be so bold as to inquire your identity?" she asked,
never changing the angle of the smile or the precision of her
speech. I introduced myself and told her that I was a new
professor in the English department.

"Oh, my dear," she fluttered, "this is indeed an occasion
of great pleasure. I—if you will permit me to introduce myself—I am Mrs. Cleo Whitecomb Hood." And she drew her-

self up to her full height, thrusting her pinched but still pretty face up at me. "Undoubtedly my reputation has preceded me to this meeting."

When I admitted apologetically that I couldn't quite place her name, the smile collapsed. She threw her head back and informed me that she was the chairman of the speech department, a well-known actress, and the wife of a former president of the college, who had now passed to his reward. I must have looked impressed, for the smile returned undimmed. Gripping my hand firmly she steered me into the building, explaining in a squeaky whisper that my prestige in the college would be greatly enhanced if she personally introduced me to my colleagues. She dragged me past the groups of people clustered in the corridor and, at the end of the hall, stopped abruptly before another woman, much taller than Mrs. Hood, apparently much older, and as gaunt and lean as a fence post. Her graying hair was processed into a neat pompadour in the front, a neat bun in the back. Mrs. Hood launched into a long and florid introduction, difficult for me to follow, but as the towering lady graciously bent to extend a wrinkled hand, I understood that she was Dr. Harder, the chairman of my department.

Her smile was already in place as she began an effusive greeting, each word selected carefully and pronounced laboriously. Mrs. Hood gripped my arm tighter, throwing me a look that indicated her sympathy at my having to listen to this doddering old woman. I didn't acknowledge the grip or the look; I was not going to be trapped into taking sides moments after my arrival in a feud so transparent and, in a small college, so potentially disastrous. Besides, there seemed little to choose between my two colleagues, although Dr. Harder's gracious-lady routine presented a more pleasant façade than the distorted grimace of Mrs. Hood's smile.

Dr. Harder concluded her formal greeting, the set speech of some kindly queen in a heroic drama, humble yet distinctly noble. Having lost her thought amid the tangle of rhetorical flourishes, I had no idea what she had said; I nodded and smiled, incapable of responding to a language I hadn't heard since, years before, I had labored through a course in Restoration drama. Dr. Harder tried to ease my confusion with an informal and personal touch.

"I know, my dear," she crooned, "that we are going to be very good friends because you have such a lovely smile. Doesn't she have a lovely smile, Mrs. Hood? Such nice white teeth."

I stood there, grinning and helpless, while Dr. Harder, still clinging to my right hand, and Mrs. Hood, gripping my left arm, smiled ever so sweetly at each other.

Someone called out that the meeting was about to begin, and with a sense of relief I allowed my colleagues to drag me between them into the meeting room.

I found a place near the back of the room and watched the other fifty or sixty members of the faculty and staff file in, stopping to shake hands and call out greetings across the room. To all appearances they were an intimate and friendly group, but it seemed strange to me that I heard no first names used. "Good to see you, Dr. So-and-so." "How was your summer, Mr. So-and-so?" The courtesy titles were pronounced carefully, with clear distinctions between the distinguished doctors and the plain old misters. When everyone had found a place on the folding chairs set up in the large lecture hall, they continued their amiable conversations, waiting for the meeting to begin. I examined the faces in the crowd—half a dozen white ones among the black—but then, aware that I was also the object of stares and furtive glances, I turned to the row of framed and faded photographs of apparently distinguished black men hung on the water-stained and peeling wall. Who were these stiff-necked men in their high starched collars and string ties? What were they famous for? Later I would ask many of my colleagues about the identity of the men in the photographs and a similar group of oil portraits that hung in the school auditorium, but no one seemed to know. Evidently, it did not matter who the men were or what they had achieved, just as long as their pictures contributed a dignified and respectable appearance.

Finally, I realized that the people around me were leaving the room. No presiding officer had begun the meeting, so after fifteen or twenty minutes everyone simply returned to the corridor, where it seemed cooler and where someone had set up a coffee urn.

Soon, however, we were hustled back into the meeting room by a short, portly man in a well-tailored dark suit. When we were all in our seats again, the meeting began— only forty-five minutes late. No one seemed to be disturbed by the tardiness; I learned quickly that lateness was the tradition, that it was unheard of at the college to commence anything on time.

A pleasant-looking black gentleman nodded to the group as he walked to the lectern and announced in a slow drawling bass that he would begin the meeting in the customary fashion by making a few opening remarks. He continued in a monotonous drone to tell us of his pleasure in having the opportunity to make the opening remarks and of his intention to keep them brief and to the point. It was appropriate that his remarks this morning be brief, he said, since he would have many other opportunities to address the group during the year.

After he had spoken for ten minutes about the intended brevity of his remarks, I tuned out the words and concentrated on watching the face perform, like watching television with the sound turned off. The masklike face preserved a dignified amiability in the constant trace of a slight smile; occasionally, it worked up an open grin and a bemused chuckle. As I watched the sequence repeated, I realized that the grin replaced the smile not through natural relaxation but through the highly self-conscious effort of a seasoned performer. With the sound tuned out, I could discern that the sequence—smile, grin, chuckle, and return to dignified seriousness—repeated itself with the regularity of a mechanical doll. I was watching a theatrical performance, and a highly skilled one, presented by an actor grown slightly weary of the part, no longer intent upon giving the appearance of spontaneity. Who was this strange man?

In his impeccable dark suit and tie he looked the part of the successful and responsible upper-middle-class American. His erect posture suggested a man who was proud of himself and his accomplishments, but there was something in his drawl that showed he knew how to carry his hat in his hand. Interested, I tuned the words back in, but I could make no sense of the florid string of abstractions and euphemisms interspersed with apparently pointless "down home" jokes. His speech was a queer mixture of pseudo-intellectual philosophizing, academic jargon, and "just plain folks" digressions. The monotony of the performance, now entering its second hour, and the heat in the poorly ventilated room made me drowsy. Yet everyone else in the room sat upright and intent, hanging on every word, smiling and chuckling when the speaker did, looking concerned and serious when the speaker did. Occasionally, members of the audience nodded in agreement and exchanged glances of approval when the speaker had made a particularly important point; but I was never able to determine the clue that triggered the approving nods, for all the remarks sounded much the same to me, and none of them made any sense. Finally, a general chorus of nods indicated that the speaker had reached a climax and I concentrated on grasping the point.

"Now then," he began, wearing the serious face again, "there is one thing which you have all heard me say many times which I will continue to say many more times, which, if you have something of significant value to utter, it cannot bear repeating often enough in sufficiency, which, as you know, when I was a teacher, was my philosophy, too, that if you said a thing in sufficiency, sooner or later, it would sink in. And so I say to you, as I say, which is that we *are* making progress."

He paused, apparently to let his remark sink in, and the members of the audience dutifully nodded approval and exchanged complacent grins of self-congratulation. So "we" apparently included them. And "progress," I gathered, was the keynote, for the speaker continued for some time to elaborate on that theme. Unfortunately, though I listened very carefully to the rest of the speech, I was not able to catch specifically what kind of progress we were making or what goal we were progressing toward. Presumably, everyone already knew what the goal was, for the audience broke into loud applause when the speaker, in conclusion, offered us his personal guarantee that if we continued to work as a team, we would reach our objective. All we had to do, he said, was accentuate the positive. It seemed simple enough—that is, if one had some basis for distinguishing the positive from the negative. But the speaker didn't go into that.

He had started to return to his seat when he remembered another item of business: the introduction of the new faculty members. He first presented the short, stocky man who had pushed us into the meeting room; this was the newly appointed dean of studies, Andrew Butler, who would address us the next day, we were told, on his philosophy of education. The speaker then called off the names of new faculty members from a list handed to him by Dean Butler. Several of those called were not present, and the speaker concluded the list with mounting anger.

"Now, you see," he said when he had finished, "that some of these people who said they would be here and which contracts have been signed for, which you can see in the files in the president's office, they are not here and present with us today on this day, when, if they are going to be here, they are supposed and required to be here."

He explained to us at some length, that the president could make plans for the coming year but could not carry them out when prospective faculty members, supposedly professional and honorable people, did not keep faith. Breaking contracts is, he said, ungentlemanly, unprofessional, illegal, and sinful; and most important, "It keeps us from making any progress." The denunciation seemed to strike everyone in the audience, and despite their innocence they shuffled out at the end of the diatribe, contrite and respectful. So he was capable of using the whip, too.

Cleo Hood trapped me at the door to ask me if I had enjoyed the opening remarks. I replied that I had been very impressed by the speaker but wondered who he was. "Oh, my dear," she shrieked in astonishment at my ignorance, "that was our beloved President Greeson."

The afternoon session of the faculty conference, like the president's opening speech, was mostly unintelligible, consisting of progress reports presented by the various school and departmental chairmen. Since they used the same meaningless jargon as the president to describe their vague progress toward some unspecified goal, I understood very little.

One or two chairmen, however, spoke clearly enough for me to understand that each department had conducted a self-study during the previous semester. The self-study was undertaken at the recommendation of several consultants sent by the regional accrediting association to help raise the standards of the school. Each of the dozen or more consultants had offered suggestions for improving the quality of instruction in the department he had inspected. Supposedly, the self-study was a follow-up to determine how well each department was complying with the recommendations of its consultant. Presumably, compliance would mean accreditation for the college. Only later would I fit the pieces together and learn just how important accreditation was to the school, but even at this meeting I came to understand that getting accredited—by hook or by crook—was "our goal," and apparently our only goal.

But in relation to that goal, the progress reports seemed doubly strange, for the chairmen devoted most of their time to explaining why they had *not* tried to comply with the consultants' recommendations. Each seemed to feel that the consultant for his department was unqualified or incompetent or both. All emphasized that the recommendations might apply to other schools, but not to "our special type of student." Everyone seemed to know what that vague phrase meant, for the faculty nodded in agreement every time "our special type of student" was used to discredit another consultant.

I arrived on the second day of the faculty conference full of questions, but there was no time to ask them. We were rushed to our seats so that a special program, designed to show the close relationship between the college and the community, might begin. The participants, two white business executives, unaware of the custom of the college, had arrived at the meeting early; and white men were not to be kept waiting. The two visitors, public relations men from the local branch of a nation-wide manufacturing company, began by telling us about their own football careers at the local Jefferson Davis High School and the state university. At that point, their position and that of the "Negro educators" in the audience was clear.

Looking just a little ill at ease among all these colored folk, they went on to recount the increasing demand in industry for trained technologists. Today, they announced, colleges all over the country face their greatest challenge—a challenge provided by the backbone of the country, American industry. It is the great task of colleges, they advised us, to train the skilled workers and technicians who will man the

industrial world of the future. Music and art and literature
have their place in a college, since they help a fellow make a
good "cultured" appearance in a job interview; but if we
wanted to prepare our students for the world of tomorrow,
we would stress math, science, and business.

So far, they assured us, the college was meeting its obliga-
tions to the future and to the business community, for it
had produced many valuable employees for the local factory.
Unfortunately, their particular factory turned out only one
key part for the corporation's machines, which were assembled elsewhere; and so far none of our graduates had
shown the necessary aptitude to be involved in the manufacturing end of the business. But to encourage us to train many
more fine graduates, their company would soon send the
college a check in the amount of one thousand dollars.

The audience smiled and applauded. The president and the
dean, looking humble and grateful, shook the hands of the
distinguished guests. The PR men, encouraged by the warm
reception their euphemisms had received, called for questions
from the floor. There were no questions. No one wanted to
put them on the spot. No one wanted to make them say
in plain English what everyone already knew: that the math
and science graduates who applied for jobs at their factory
were handed a broom and a can of Drāno. If we gave offense,
they might not send the check. After all, a thousand dollars
is a thousand dollars.

We adjourned for luncheon in the school cafeteria, steak
at the head table for the administrators and their guests,
hamburger at the faculty tables. It was time for the dean of
studies to deliver his formal statement of beliefs to the
faculty. When we were halfway through the vanilla ice cream,
he rose nervously in his place between the two clean-cut, all-
American PR men and plunged into his memorized speech.
The words came rapidly, crisply. He was the general address-
ing the troops, the business executive addressing the board

of directors. His whole manner was self-consciously firm, then vehement, as he leaned further out over the head table. He loomed over the startled audience, waving his hands and at last pounding the table with his fist and shouting angrily that he believed above all things in "academic excellence." "I tell you *that* is most important," he bellowed. He smashed his fist on the table again, rattling the silverware against the plates, and the words of his creed rushed out in a violent torrent: "I tell you I believe in discipline of the mind, spiritual development, and the building of character. And I tell you that is what we will all believe in so long as I am dean of Thomas College." Then he suddenly collapsed into his chair, his round face bathed in perspiration. The PR men clapped, the faculty took it up, and Dean Butler bowed humbly to the audience.

The style was frenetic, but the words were much the same as the president's. What did all those fine phrases mean? Did "spiritual development" mean straightening your hair and wearing a Brooks Brothers suit and sitting down to break bread with the white businessmen who gave you money but who would not give your students a decent job? What was the difference between mental discipline and moral suicide? What is the "character" of a slave? Confused and depressed, I sat watching my melted ice cream creep to the edge of the plate and drip slowly onto the starched white tablecloth.

The faculty conference dragged on through another day of ornate and meaningless rhetoric. No one seemed to say what he meant or to mean what he said. I gathered what little information I could, a few bits of flotsam on a sea of words. But my new notebook lay blank and useless in my lap, and I left the last meeting as I had entered the first, not knowing how to order a book or requisition a pencil, not knowing what classes I would teach or when or where. But if the faculty conference was not for the purpose of providing information to the faculty, what was it for? The boredom and frustration of three days of listening suddenly hit me; I felt weary, haggard, and enormously depressed. My mind wandered to the slogan of my former riding instructor, a hard, hatchet-faced little man whom I had both feared and hated: "The quickest way to gentle a horse is to beat him senseless."

The faculty conference meetings struck the first blow at self-respect and self-determination, but the administration had other ingenious means of putting faculty—particularly new faculty—in their place. The three days of faculty orientation were followed immediately by the four-day student registration period, at which all faculty members were required to work. New faculty members, however, could do little real work during registration since they were unfamiliar with college curricula and course requirements, and the college had not given them this information. (Many new teachers had asked the college during the previous summer to send them course catalogues and timetables, and although they were advised that the information would be sent "when available," they never received it; the obsolete catalogue was still "in process of revision," and the timetable had been thrown together at the last minute.) In response to the questions of a student, therefore, the new teacher could only refer him to one of the senior faculty members. After four days of saying, "I'm sorry but you will have to ask Dr. So-and-so," the new teacher himself came to regard Dr. So-and-so as a powerful authority. And, because so many students wanted it, Dr. So-and-so's trivial information about physical-education requirements began to seem enormously important.

Broken down by the faculty conference and the grueling registration period, new teachers were not prepared to quibble over their teaching assignments, although these, too, were used to humble them. Teaching assignments in most departments were handed out by the chairman on the basis of seniority, wth the longest tenured members of the department selecting the courses they wanted to teach and the newcomers scraping up the leftovers. In assigning courses, few department chairmen considered the training and specialization of their various faculty members. Few even bothered to consult new teachers, but simply handed them a list of the classes they were to teach. In many departments, older, poorly qualified teachers chose advanced courses as a kind of status symbol, leaving introductory or remedial courses to younger teachers. In the English department, this policy meant that freshman composition and remedial grammar were taught by the two youngest faculty members, both trained in literature rather than remedial instruction, while the advanced literature courses in the young teachers' specialties were taught by senior faculty who had little advanced training and, in some cases, were unfamiliar with the course material. To see one's own favorite subjects botched by an uninterested colleague is frustrating enough, but to be assigned courses one feels ill prepared to teach is mortifying. That, of course, is one intent of the teaching assignment policy. The new teacher is effectively restrained from the sin of intellectual pride—and from the joy of intellectual activity.

Many other methods of keeping new faculty in their place as underlings were petty but effective. As a rule, new teachers were not invited to faculty social events given by administrators, although a few invitations were addressed to those new teachers who fully cooperated with institutional policy, who evinced the greatest promise of becoming loyal retainers. Similarly, new teachers were assigned by the president to the most meaningless of faculty committees, committees that met only rarely to ratify the chair's decisions, or not at all. They also were summoned to the campus to perform menial chores such as sorting library books or fashioning homecoming decorations.

One of the most effective of these seemingly trivial techniques was "name stripping," the deliberate omission or distortion of a teacher's name. The president and the dean of studies often mailed to new teachers memos and notices on which the teacher's name was misspelled or otherwise altered; the name Jones might become Johns, Johnson, Jonas, Jeans, Jos, or any of a dozen other variations. When the last name was spelled correctly, the first name would be distorted. Titles, too, were tampered with in this way, with Dr. becoming Mrs. or even Mr., so that not only one's status but also one's gender was transformed. Frequently, in a refinement of this practice with some strong racist overtones, my name was wholly or partially interchanged with that of the only other white woman on the faculty; I became Carol Jones while she became Ann Dexter. Name stripping also was played as a verbal game; even in personal conversation, administrators mixed up the names of new teachers. After we had been on the campus for nine months the president and his wife still pretended to think that I was Dr. Dexter and Dr. Dexter was Dr. Jones. A black colleague with whom I had often worked asked me at the end of the year, *"Which one* are you?" A variation on this name game was the pretense that one was not acquainted with a new teacher at all; some new teachers, after months on campus, still had to identify themselves monthly at the pay-roll office in order to get their checks. Clerical and secretarial staff took as much delight in the game as did the top administrators, for it was an effective way of showing professors how unimportant they were. So the game was played enthusiastically, used by administrators against faculty and by one group of institutional inmates against another. Name stripping, of course, was based on the premise that to deny a person's name is to deny his existence. Deprived of individual identity, one may try to regain it by becoming an important member of the group, by compelling the group to acknowledge his value to them.

Within the context of a closed institution, however, one becomes valuable only insofar as he does the institution's bidding. When a new Thomas faculty member manifested promise of becoming a safe Uncle Tom, he received his party invitation with his title and full name spelled correctly. Until then, he remained a nameless invisible man.

The students, even more completely than the faculty, were inmates of the institution. Like the faculty, they had to be broken in. New freshmen and transfer students were brought to the campus for a preschool orientation session so the college could indoctrinate them before they met any grumbling upperclassmen. The new students arrived in a state of exhaustion induced by the emotional excitement of their first real trip away from home and the physical strain of a long, arduous bus ride. Crowded into small dormitory rooms, each with three or four other newcomers, they got little rest before the first day-long session of placement testing. The testing procedure continued for most of the orientation period, with no explanation of its purpose. Many of the tests administered to the new students apparently *had* no purpose, for their results were not used in placement or evaluation and in some cases were not even tabulated until months after the tests had been given. But the students suffered through fearful days, thinking that if they failed the tests they would be sent home in disgrace. Examinations put the best of students under an emotional strain; to students with a long record of mediocre academic performance, they can be intensely demoralizing. At Thomas the tests served both to demoralize the newcomer and to let him know that he was on trial, that he would have to earn acceptance on Thomas's terms. The student's humiliation was intensified when he recognized that he had done badly on all the exams, for he could not have known that almost all Thomas students do badly on such standardized tests. He was left, then, with the sense of his own isolated failure.

When the rest of the student body arrived for the general orientation, the whole group was welcomed by the president and other administrators. The college's official spokesmen talked at length about the aims of the school, its Christian atmosphere, its high achievement; but they offered no more practical information to the students than they had supplied to the faculty. Such meetings only added to the confusion of the new students and to their sense of inferiority, for clearly the newcomers had not been important enough to warrant a presidential address of their own.

The orientation period was followed by four days of registration, during which the students were supposed to sign up officially for the courses they wished to attend. The fact that it took at least four full days to register a student body consisting of about 500 people suggests the confusion of the whole procedure; many large universities manage to register accurately 20,000 or 30,000 students in less time than it took Thomas to process a far smaller number. But if registration was a time of confusion for upperclassmen, for the freshmen it was a period of utter panic. Each student was given a pamphlet of instructions which admonished him first to obtain a Permit to Register from the vice-president and an Admission to Register from the registrar. Next he was to work out a trial schedule of the courses he wished to take. The college catalogue, however, was so ambiguously worded that it was almost impossible to figure out the course requirements for any given program, and the course descriptions, which had not been revised for years, often bore little resemblance to the actual content of the courses offered. The college timetable, listing the hours at which each course would be offered, contained so many errors that a feasible class schedule could not be determined from it; and often two basic courses, both of which freshmen were required to take, were apparently given at the same hour.

If, despite these handicaps, the student managed to work

out a trial schedule, he was then warned by the registration pamphlet that he "must obtain counseling from [his] Academic Major and Minor Advisers." The signatures of the advisers, he was told, "must be affixed to all forms." Unfortunately, the freshman had neither major nor minor adviser and probably didn't even understand what the the terms *major* and *minor* meant. If he consulted the college catalogue for assistance, he discovered that in many subjects he was required to complete two years of work before he would be allowed to specify a major field. Yet he was warned that he needed for registration not only the signatures of his major and minor advisers, but also the signatures of the department chairmen in his major and minor fields. In addition, he was ordered to obtain endorsements from the instructor of each course he wished to take, although many instructors had been listed incorrectly in the timetable and several were not present at registration time. Next, the student had to collect approving signatures from the dean of studies, the registrar, and the director of admissions. The freshman, of course, knew none of these people by sight and consequently might spend hours inquiring the identity and whereabouts of this or that instructor or official. Most of the freshmen finally crumbled when it came to getting the signature of the director of admissions, for the college *had* no director of admissions. Finally, the distraught student was directed to report to the assessor—another nonexistent officer—and then to the cashier.

Registration thus was a formidable procedure, made even more nerve-racking for the novice by the repeated warnings of the pamphlet: "Do Not Detach Forms!" "It Is Necessary That Forms Be Attached." "Do Not Write with One Carbonized Form on Top of Another!" "Do Not Use Pencil or Fountain Pen!" "Do Not Fold, Staple, or Mutilate Forms!" "Forms That Are Folded, Stapled, or Mutilated Will Not Be Accepted!" "Print! Do Not Write!" The pamphlet further warned that each student would be given only one set of forms; any additional forms he required—as a result of his carelessness or inability to follow instructions —would have to be purchased at the rate of fifteen cents each. Finally, he was warned that "failure to abide by the afore-mentioned instructions will result in the student's not being granted credit for any course he may attend regardless of the amount of time he may have attended the course." The paralyzing prospect of toiling through a year of college classes only to have one's mistakes in registration discovered and one's credit erased at the last minute made it an act of extraordinary bravery to put ballpoint pen to paper, marking ineradicably those awesome, gleaming, blank, carbonized forms.

The freshmen had no advisers, and since they registered in advance of the upperclassmen, they could not appeal to older students for help. Wandering around the littered reg-istration tables in the library, sweating from fear as much as from the August heat, they wheedled information from random faculty members on what courses they were to take and whose signatures they were to obtain, but the orders of one teacher might be countermanded by a teacher from an-other department with competing interests. As the anxious students tried to piece together a picture of what was expected of them, they were subjected to a steady stream of insults from faculty members resentful of having to spend four days registering students. Teachers, seated in relative comfort at their tables, accused the exhausted students of wasting their valuable professorial time. They sternly corrected students who failed to add the proper "ma'am" or "sir" when address-ing a teacher and silenced them for speaking before being spoken to. A few black teachers commented freely and loudly on the "ugliness" of the blackest of the students and the "beauty" of those light-skinned girls who obviously had "a lot of Indian blood."

"Speak up, boy. What? What? Quit that mumbling. I haven't got all day to spend on you."

"Can you tell me where is . . ."

"Haven't you any manners, boy? Didn't your mama teach you to say 'please'?"

"Please, can you . . ."

" 'Please'! Please what? Who do you think you're talkin' to, boy?"

"Please, ma'am . . ."

"That's better. Well, don't stand there gawkin', boy. Speak up. And don't slouch. Stand up straight, boy."

"Yes, ma'am. Please, ma'am, can you tell me where is it I sign up for Math 1?"

"Math! Math! This is the English department table, boy."

"Yes, ma'am. I knowed that, but . . ."

"I *knew* that, boy. I *knew* that. Well, what are you wasting my time for? Can't you read? You'll never get through college! And press your pants, boy. You look a sight."

"Yes, ma'am. Thank you, ma'am."

"Wait a minute, boy. Here's a dime. Go get me a cup of coffee. With two sugars. And don't be all day about it, either. Now, that's a good boy."

Few students succeeded in registering on the first day; they were forced to try again on the second and third and fourth days of registration. Many left the library in tears.

During his first week on campus, the student also was subjected to many other indignities. Whatever privacy he may have known in his own home disappeared in the overcrowded dormitory rooms and bathrooms in which shower and toilet stalls often lacked doors. His closet and even his suitcase might be ransacked by a dormitory matron or by curious roommates who would appropriate choice toilet articles for their own use. All young women were obliged to be in their rooms, present and accounted for, each evening at the same time. All students had to eat together in the overcrowded cafeteria, eating the prescribed menu at the prescribed time or going hungry.

"Move along. Move along. Where's your meal ticket, boy? Have it ready. You're holdin' up the line. Take a tray. Take a tray. Ain't nobody here to wait on you."

"Please, ma'am. Can I get two of them little sausages?"

"Two sausages! Who you think you are, boy? You'll take what you gets. Keep movin.' "

Meanwhile, each newcomer's right to withhold or disclose himself disintegrated under a barrage of questions from deans, counselors, and business officers about his family life and financial standing.

At the same time, incoming students lost their names, temporarily at least, and were addressed by many adults on campus as "you," "boy," "honey," or just plain "Hey, nigger." They quickly learned that they were subject to the discipline —and the insults—of any adult at the school; the lowliest secretary or janitor, by virtue of his seniority in years and in service to the institution, was free to command any student; and many staff employees, having no other author- ity, freely indulged their right to dispatch students on mean- ingless errands.

A very few students who could not tolerate this invasion of the self took the only alternative open to them: they went home in disgust. But most of them had already learned, by growing up black, that they had very few rights. They had learned the ABC's of the southern Negro: Accept, Behave, and Care about the white man more than about yourself. No one needed to teach them humility, though they were to receive some brutal lessons at Thomas. Yet Thomas, for most of them, represented their only chance to fulfill their modest, and often pathetic, dreams of a better life than they had known. One freshman girl wrote:

A good life is life that you had everything that you want like a beautiful brick home with an air condition, all the money you want, a good hard working husband. I amn't greed; I want money but I am satisfy with what I have and that will go for husband when I get him.

So, in order to get the money or the husband, they swallowed the insults and remained hopefully at Thomas.

They remained to learn, as the semester wore on, that their every act was subject to official approval. To stay in bed when ill, a student needed written permission from the nurse. To attend a family funeral, a student needed permission from the dean of student affairs. To buy a book or a bar of soap in the school store, he needed the approval of the store manager, who might review the details of his bill in the presence of other student customers. Even in picking up his mail from home at the school post office, the student was usually forced to exchange obscenities with the part-time minister who served as postmaster; female students had to endure being the object of his innuendos.

"Well, look who's here. What you want, honey? You think somebody's gone and wrote you a love letter? Hot little thing like you oughta get a load of 'em."

"Please, reverend, can I get my letters?"

"Honey, you just step around here and I'll give you some letters you never seen before!"

Mature students—mothers, war veterans—had to ask a teacher's permission to leave the classroom to go to the toilet; and sometimes permission was denied, on the grounds that they should have tended to such matters "on their own time."

Exerting such control over the minutiae of life, the college found it unnecessary to take stands on more important issues. The president of the student council once wished to write to Ralph Ellison, who was scheduled to speak at a neighboring college, inviting the distinguished author to visit the Thomas campus. The letter was never posted, however, because the young man could not obtain permission from the dean of student affairs to use official college stationery and postage stamps for his letter. The student, a senior, was so used to accepting such restrictions that he never realized that the college was employing this excuse to exclude a prospective (and, from the administration's point of view, controversial) speaker from the campus; he thought they were only regulating the supply of paper and postage stamps. And even when I offered the student a typewriter, official stationery, and stamps, he refused them because he did not have "permission."

The students also learned the rules governing personal appearance; they had to be neatly dressed at all times. For the female students, the unwritten rules called for the wearing of dresses (or skirts) and hose, a code that in the hot southern climate, at certain times of the year, amounted to mortification of the flesh. When the temperature soared above 100° and I perspired in sundress and sandals, young women in my classes suffered physical torments under their layers of stockings, girdles, petticoats, and Sunday dresses. The classes could not leave the stifling classrooms to meet under a shady tree, however, because the women students were too dressed up to sit on the grass. And in the continuous rains of winter, when the red mud crept up the ankles of my knee-high boots, they hobbled to class in their high-heeled shoes. In that climate, the dress policy could not have been more onerous if it had required the constant wearing of hair shirts and thorns, but the students accepted it as a matter of course, and even with gratitude—for dressing up in their best clothes was one last means of asserting who they were. Stripped of name, station, dignity, identity, they could still array themselves in those material symbols of themselves and even be commended for doing so. Once, when the fire alarm rang in a girls' dormitory, many of the girls—not knowing it was a false alarm—stayed in the building, nevertheless, to pack their clothes. It was as though they, themselves, without their fine garments, were not worth saving. They had learned the lessons of orientation well.

Some students sought to preserve their identity by maintaining their ties with home, but they had to have written permission from their parents to return home for a visit; and in most cases the expense of transportation home put a visit, except for the Christmas holidays, out of the question. A student might phone his parents—if the parents had a phone—but again the expense was often prohibitive. Even getting a letter from home involved an unpleasant encounter with the postmaster. It often was easier for students to try to forget about home—at least until Christmas.

So the ties with home, and with the world outside the gates, were quickly and effectively cut. The student became an inmate of the college. On campus, he had difficulty regaining the identity he had lost. He made a few friends among the other students, but the people who mattered—the people in authority—scarcely noticed him. His teachers did not bother to learn his name, finding it easier to address him —and all his fellows—as "boy" or, in the case of young women, "honey." His counselor only summoned him to reprimand him for his absence from class. He found it hard to establish *himself* in any area of his life, for suddenly all the areas overlapped. He might try to present himself, as *he* saw himself, to his dormitory matron, his athletic coach, a certain teacher, the cafeteria staff, or a dean, but he soon discovered that the dormitory matron, the coach, the teacher, the cafeteria workers, and the dean all got together over coffee, and *they*—not he—determined who he was.

If the adults on campus bothered to speak to the student at all, it was to dispatch him on an errand or to scold him for his appearance or his grammar. The chairman of the speech department hung a sign over her office door: "Abandon all incorrect English, Ye who enter here." If a student spoke a dialect, as almost all of the students did (so did the speech department chairman when she became excited and forgot to plan "correct" sentences), he simply could not speak to that professor, either out of class or in it. A student who heard rumors that "Black Is Beautiful" and let his hair go "natural" might find himself unwelcome in some quarters until he again pressed his "nappy" hair.

"Linda," I told a student one day, "I really liked the natural you were wearing last week. You looked just beautiful. Why did you press your hair again?"

"Oh, well, I had to," she replied. "I thought it looked pretty good too, but my dorm matron, she wrote my mother a letter about it, tellin' her how awful I looked and all. My mother, she called me up and told me to press my hair. She was scared they was goin' to put me outa school."

All the invasions of privacy, the petty rules, the insults and humiliations stripped the student of whatever identity he may have had. He became a nonperson, fearful of the awesome authority above him—and fearful that the authority might not accept him. He learned to play the game.

Among other things, he learned which infractions bring punishment. If he failed to keep the prescribed dormitory hours, he would be confined to his room. If he did not display subservience to his teachers, he would receive low grades. If he broke any of the myriad rules, he would get a dressing down from *some* adult. He learned, too, the behavior that brings reward. Punishment at Thomas is so common, however, that "reward" usually means simply the absence of punishment. Nothing very bad happens to the student so long as he speaks (in the presence of adults) only when spoken to and does the bidding of every adult. His success at playing the game dictated by the institution determines whether and how long he will be permitted to stay. His whole future hangs upon his being what the adults in his world expect him to be.

Struggling to meet the expectations of adults is, of course, the problem of most youngsters at some stage in their life. But for most young people in the white middle class, the struggle is to come up to the high demands of parents and teachers. Few stigmas are as great as that of being an under-achiever. The problem for Thomas students is different. While they are expected to come up to certain superficial standards of posture, grooming, and manners, their main struggle is to "come down," to repress, to keep silent, to be passive, to be—as much as possible—invisible.

So, from his status as nonperson, the student begins to build the character prescribed for him. The adult attitudes and rules imply that he is a child, totally without the capacity for intelligent choice and responsible behavior. The student, in response, becomes lazy, passive, irresponsible, subservient, and—to protect what remains of himself—covert. He becomes a child, a stereotypical "Sambo," a "nigger."

Indeed, orientation had made niggers of us all. Of course, all colleges have orientation meetings for new faculty and students; recognizing that the transition to a new school for a faculty member, or from high school to college for a student, may be difficult, colleges smooth the way with informational sessions. But Thomas, being a peculiar institution, used these familiar procedures for its own ends: to humble its new inmates. To an outsider—a consultant or an inspector—such "standard procedures" appeared on paper both normal and creditable. To the new student and teacher entering into institutional life, however, the procedures were unexpected, irrational, and devastating. Yet, as the conditioning inexorably continued, the new inmate, confused and humbled, saw the rationale, the intrinsic logic of the system itself. Trying to adapt himself to the world of the college, entering the closed institution, he entered the absurd. And as ties to the larger world were cut, one by one, the absurd began to make perfectly good sense.

4

The Masters

Power, at Thomas, apparently lies with President Greeson, the amiable though slightly incoherent gentleman who had addressed the faculty conference. He had grown up in the area, graduated from the college as a young man, and returned as Dr. Greeson to join the administration. Just where he had earned his master's degree and doctorate in education he never disclosed to me. And fond as he was of reminiscing about his years as a teacher—to indicate to the faculty that he knew more about teaching than they did—he never mentioned where or what he had taught.

He wore his power with studied casualness, pausing in his walks across the campus to exchange greetings with students, dropping by the faculty office building to chat about the weather and make sure "everything" was "all right." And he always had a folksy anecdote to relate. Yet there was something in the stiffness of his walk—as though he were constantly marching in an academic procession—that let you know he was different. His precise use of courtesy titles and the superficiality of his conversation warned you that he was distant, unapproachable. He came off as a man who humbly accepted his own greatness, as one who wanted us to know that he would be very much like the rest of us—were it not for his inescapable destiny.

His public performances were staged at carefully spaced intervals, just often enough to keep the college in mind of his greatness, but not so frequently that his image diminished through overexposure. Reportedly, he spent most of his time at his desk behind a placard that proclaimed in gilt Gothic letters, "Dr. Simon L. Greeson, President." At faculty meetings he liked to boast that from his office window he could observe, at any time of day, precisely where all his faculty members were and what they were doing. The brag preyed on guilty consciences and was accepted with fearful faith; the president was credited with occult powers. At all times, the venetian blinds at the president's office window were kept partially closed; from the outside one saw only that opaque screen. But inside, with an unobstructed view of everyone, lurked the president, peeking out—or so the faculty felt, even when he was actually hundreds of miles away on a fund-raising junket. Affable, folksy, paternal President Greeson gave everyone the jitters.

Most of the faculty and staff had good reason to fear President Greeson, for he had absolute authority over contracts. He alone decided whether one could keep his job or not, and few members of the Thomas College "family" could afford to lose their jobs. Many of the office staff members were young women who had grown up in the community and graduated from the college. They lived in the security of home, and nobody demanded much of them on the job. They had comfortable berths and a lifetime meal ticket, if they kept their eyes open and their mouths shut. They knew it and behaved accordingly.

It was the faculty who had most to lose and who were most intimidated by Greeson's power over their careers.

Many were nearing or past the usual retirement age, too old to find teaching jobs elsewhere and too tired to begin life again in a new community. Others were poorly qualified. Padded credentials that looked good in the Thomas College catalogue would not easily pass the examination of a hiring committee at another college. And at a time when Ph.D.'s were begging for jobs, teachers with only questionable M.A.'s had little hope in the job market. Still others had husbands or wives employed at the college or in the community. If one of them lost a college position, both might have to find new jobs in another town, a task that made the thought of moving doubly forbidding. Several faculty members who were qualified for other and better jobs remained tied to Thomas by aged parents, mortgaged homes, the prestige they enjoyed as "big men," or dedication to their students.

Job security concerns college teachers everywhere, but most have some safeguards against arbitrary dismissal. The tenure system, for example, has many drawbacks, but it supposedly does protect the right of faculty who have passed their probationary period to speak out on campus issues without inordinate fear of reprisal. Even probationary faculty members may sometimes be shielded from capricious firing by a local chapter of the American Association of University Professors or a campus faculty senate. Even where such bodies have only advisory powers, the knowledge that unjust treatment of faculty may be investigated and publicized is often enough to temper the action of administrators. And increasingly, college teachers are turning to labor unions to ensure fair administrative practices.

The Thomas College faculty, however, is protected by none of these safeguards. Since the college is not accredited, it cannot have a recognized AAUP chapter. Occasionally, in the past, there has been some radical talk of organizing a faculty senate, but President Greeson's assurance that no need for a senate exists was enough to squelch the idea. That the suggestion came from the few young white and Northern black faculty members—usually transient and always suspect to the older black instructors—didn't increase its popularity. Unionizing, of course, was unthinkable in a city from which even blue-collar unions had been almost completely excluded by local industrialists. In any case, the black teacher would not easily give up his traditional prestige as a "professional" in the black community.

Thus, at Thomas, the tenure system is, in theory, the only security faculty members have. In fact, it provides no security at all. According to the college faculty guide, written by President Greeson, "faculty members are employed for a period of three years on a probationary basis." During this period, "each teacher must prove himself" by demonstrating:

1. Adequacy in his academic field and in the classroom
2. High moral character
3. Ongoing advancement by attending school to improve academically
4. Capacity for working in cooperation with faculty and students
5. Contributions to the educational advancement of the college through research

After three years, teachers who have proved themselves to the satisfaction of the president and "who have satisfactorily completed the probationary requirements will be given continuous tenure status."

The achievement of continuous tenure status, however, does not alter a teacher's precarious position. He still receives his contract yearly, each contract covering the ten-month period of the regular school term, with no assurance that he will be accorded preference over probationers for summer-school teaching. Like probationary faculty, he is still subject to dismissal for:

1. Incompetency

2. Unprofessional conduct
3. Dereliction of duty
4. Physical and mental impairment
5. Immorality
6. Any other act that may be detrimental to the college

And in all cases, the president is the sole judge of the teacher's competency, professional conduct, morality, and "other acts." Although the faculty guide assures all dismissed teachers of "recourse to appeal," no genuine appeal is possible. Recourse to appeal means simply that the teacher, if he can get an appointment, may argue the matter in person with President Greeson, the man who decided to fire the teacher in the first place.

Continuous tenure status does not even entitle the teacher to advance warning of his impending dismissal. A teacher who knows months ahead of time that he will not be asked to return has nothing to lose in speaking his mind. The college cannot risk that threat to its complacency, so it retains its key weapon—next year's contract—to give or withhold at the last possible moment. Thus, the tenured teacher, like the probationer, usually learns of his dismissal in late April or early May, when contracts are issued and his is not among them. Since most colleges hire their September faculty during the preceding winter and early spring, it is too late for the teacher fired in May to get a job—unless he is willing to take the leavings.

The dismissal of a tenured professor, however, may be more abrupt than the simple failure of the college to renew his contract. Like the campus maintenance men, he can be fired at any time during the year on five minutes' notice. And President Greeson, for all his outward affability, has a notorious temper. There have been cases of professors entering Greeson's office and leaving hurriedly without their jobs.

It is not that President Greeson enforces all the faculty

guide rules. Far from it. Every student knows that there are tenured professors of long standing on the campus who are incompetent; either they do not know their subject matter, or they can't teach it—or both. There are those who neglect their duties in favor of more lucrative sideline hustles. The conduct of many who seek power and undermine their fellows could not be called professional. There are foreign professors whose English is unintelligible to the students. And there are the ancient and the senile. Yet some of these professors, however, retain their positions from year to year, while very good teachers are let go. Perhaps it is only coincidence that the dismissed teachers have often been critical of the administration; or perhaps criticism of the administration constitutes "unprofessional conduct" and is itself grounds for dismissal. In any case, the regulations clearly exist only to provide Greeson with paper justification for his arbitrary decisions. The tenure system, then, is only an illusion, a theoretical fantasy that can be written down in an official booklet to give the college the appearance of an educational institution.

So complete is Greeson's authority over contracts that a dismissed professor may not even be told why he is being dismissed. Greeson does not have to defend his decision to any board of appeal; he may not even have to defend it to himself. In April of our first year at the college, Dr. Norden, an outspoken young Northern black woman and an associate professor of English, was summoned to Dean Butler's office and told that she would not be rehired. She asked for an explanation and was told only that she would receive a letter from the president. She waited for her letter, remembering the statement in the faculty guide: "Any person dismissed for justifiable cause will receive a written explanation telling why he is being discharged." In May she received her dismissal letter from the president; it stated merely that her services "would not be required in future" and thanked her for "services rendered." Obviously, the letter explained nothing. Unable to gain admittance to Greeson's office, she went to Dean Butler to demand the reasons for her dismissal.

"Well, you see," he stammered, "the accrediting board insists—insists—that we have more doctors of philosophy. We can't use doctors of education; we must have doctorates in philosophy if we are going to get accredited, and so you see it is in the interests of the future of . . . ."

"Dean Butler," Dr. Norden interrupted, "my credentials are in your files. If you will look at them, you will see that I hold a Ph.D."

Butler stuttered, shuffled his papers, and, finally, seeing that there was no other way to get her out of his office, promised that he would call the matter to the president's attention. Together they would review her credentials. Yes, they would consider that teachers with only master's degrees were being retained while she was being "let go." Yes, there apparently had been a slip-up somewhere. They would tend to it immediately and let her know right away. But Dr. Norden understood that she had spoken once too often against administration policy, and she left Butler's office knowing that she would not hear from him again.

Dr. Norden was only a probationer, but Mr. Costa, the Spanish professor, had tenure. Nevertheless, he didn't get a contract either. Nor did he get an explanation of the reasons for his dismissal. Costa was an unassuming old man, quiet and hard working. He had few suggestions and little energy for innovations and curriculum development. But he knew his subject matter—Spanish was his native language—and he taught it well. As a result, his students were devoted to him. The students in Costa's one-man department, when they heard of his dismissal, drew up a petition in his behalf, an unheard-of act of defiance. President Greeson, as usual, was inaccessible, so the student leaders took their petition to Butler, asking that the administration at least inform Mr.

Costa of the reasons for his dismissal. They were told that there was indeed "good reason" for getting rid of Costa, but the reason could not be stated, even to Costa himself, because it was "too embarrassing." A few of the students left Butler's office thoroughly disgusted with the administration's smear tactics, but most came away speculating on what little Mr. Costa could have done that was too dreadful even to talk about.

Yet Mr. Costa may not have lost his job altogether. The president knows that Costa, old and weary as he is, will not find another position and leave town. In August, Costa will still be around, unemployed. To fire a tenured professor in the spring and rehire him as a new probationer in the fall, at a much lower salary, is economical; and it certainly helps keep the faculty in its place.

Theoretically, of course, the president is not supposed to have all that power. On paper, the president is supposed to cooperate with department and school chairmen and with the dean of studies in recruiting, promoting, and firing faculty members. And when it is convenient for him to do so, Greeson may share the responsibility for a personnel decision with some chairman who is willing to be his unwitting accomplice. If his decision is opposed by the chairman of a concerned department, however, he simply acts unilaterally. Without consulting the chairman of the physical education department, Greeson fired his protégé and then paid so little attention to the chairman's protest that he was forced to resort to writing a "student petition" and coercing physical education majors to sign in a desperate effort to keep his ally on the pay roll. The physical education chairman, the coach of winning teams, had more than his share of prestige; his petition was merely shrugged off, while a similar effort by another department chairman probably would have ended in the firing of the chairman, too.

In selecting new faculty, Greeson also exercised absolute

power. He sometimes let department chairmen go through the motions of interviewing prospects, but no one had the authority or even the information to discuss salary except Greeson. Since it is impossible to persuade anyone to accept a job without knowing what his salary will be, all decisions rested with Greeson. A chairman might report to the president that he had a couple of fine prospects for his department ready to talk about salary only to find that Greeson had already hired someone for the job.

To maintain his position of power, Greeson needs the help of one man. To hold the underlings—faculty and students—in awe of him, he must preserve a certain aloofness, a dignified distance, like the puppeteer who manipulates the Punch and Judy show from above. Underlings who are manipulated and deprived of their rights characteristically become resentful and angry. The truly skillful puppeteer learns how to manipulate not only the people but their anger as well, deflecting it away from himself to some secondary object.

Displaced anger is common to all people. The man reprimanded by his boss goes home to yell at his wife; the schoolboy punished by the teacher kicks the dog. But perhaps it is more common among black Americans, who, during most of their history in this country, have expressed anger against their primary oppressor, the white man, only at the risk of their lives. In any case, displaced anger is the prevailing emotion at Thomas College, for President Greeson has set up a convenient scapegoat. In ante-bellum days, the plantation slaves often hated the overseer, the ever-present man with the whip, more than their aloof, impersonal owner. And just as the owner needed his overseer to run the risk of taking personal control over the slaves, President Greeson needed his overseer, the dean of studies.

At the time, the dean of studies happened to be Andrew

Butler, an old acquaintance whom Greeson had somehow seduced to the college. But the identity of the dean didn't really matter; it was the office that was important. For years the college had been able to retain a dean for no more than one or two years. Most remained only one year, but some—the duller ones—took two years to catch on. The men, however, were dispensable. As long as there was someone labeled "Dean" to conduct faculty meetings, chair committees, enforce rules, and issue directives, the president could sit safely above the battle. The faculty and students would spend much of their time being angry with each other and most of it being angry with the dean. And many of the naive would wonder aloud why in the world the president had hired such a man.

Clearer heads understood why the president had hired Butler. The dean was a gullible fool. Vain, ambitious, and self-deluded, he played the part as though he, and not the president, had designed it for him. No one ever knew exactly where Greeson had known Butler; reportedly they had served together at another school before Greeson assumed the presidency of Thomas. But Greeson, anticipating the annual vacancy in the dean's office, had been trying for a long time to recruit Butler. Finally, he had succeeded, presumably with the enticement of a very high salary plus an excellent salary for Butler's wife, a highly qualified history professor. The real inducement, however, was probably not the salary but the promise of administrative prestige.

Butler came to Thomas College from a position as speech professor at one of the better black colleges. He held a fine job at a respected school, undoubtedly at a comfortable salary—but he was still only a teacher. Then, too, there was the problem of his wife: beautiful, well educated, intelligent, and hip. The black man in America has always been troubled by the black woman's ability to get a job more easily and to make more money than he; that is one of the emas-

culating devices built into the social system. Poor Butler
had gone to all the trouble of getting a doctorate and becoming a college professor—and there he was with a woman
better educated than himself and probably at least as well
paid. Surely, for him there must be a higher calling. The
call came from Thomas College, and the lowly professor
became a powerful dean.

The fact that he had no previous experience as an administrator didn't matter much; given his personality, Butler
probably would have made the same mistakes in any case.
His aims were laudable but scarcely realistic, the product of
his vanity, not of his intelligence. From the outset, he saw
himself as a big-timer come to the small college in the small
town to set it straight. Single-handedly he would reform
the system, introducing order, efficiency, enlightenment to
Thomas College. He would modernize administration, inspire faculty, and attract new and better students. In his
vanity, nothing was beyond his daring. If need be, he would
not hesitate to rock the boat. He did not know that he had
been hired as ballast—and ballast he would be.

He began, in his initial address to the faculty on his
philosophy of education, on a messianic note. He left no
doubt about his high ideals: discipline of the mind, forming
of the character, and the like. But like all messiahs, he was
an emotional exhorter. He was not an intellectual man. He
wasn't equipped to examine his shibboleths. It simply never
occurred to him to ask what phrases like "discipline of the
mind" meant. How does one discipline a mind? To what
system? And how does one recognize a disciplined mind or
a formed character when he comes across them? Obviously
Butler knew the answer to that. A disciplined mind and
a formed character meant a mind and character very much
like his own. Unfortunately, no one—least of all Butler himself—fully understood what Butler's mind and character
were like.

In the make-up of his character, vanity vied with ambition. It was an uneasy competition. While vanity dictated reform, ambition dictated collaboration with the system. His vanity had bought a large house and decorated it luxuriously; his ambition whispered that it was President Greeson who had hired him and who could fire him. His vanity assured him he could change the college; his ambition cautioned him that when President Greeson, many years his senior, retired, he could inherit it. And so he vacillated, encouraging reform and then stifling it, advocating changes and then undermining them. And usually it was the students who suffered.

Take the case of Butler's honors program, a project he devised at the end of the first semester. He had known from the outset that his future career in administration, his hope of moving up to bigger and better colleges, depended upon his making significant improvements at Thomas. During the first few months of his administration, however, he had found the college maddeningly resistant to change. It was the president or the vice-president, with his budget, who usually stood in the way of the dean's grandiose schemes, but since Butler was incapable of admitting to himself that he was being used, he had to place the blame elsewhere. He blamed the students. It was Thomas's "special type of student"—the "dummy"— who was holding back his career. So he got it into his head that if he could attract "a higher type of student" to Thomas, the college would automatically improve and his future would be assured.

Throughout the first semester, the dean had engaged in a running argument with Dr. Norden. She maintained that the college underestimated and patronized its students, offering them so little stimulation that they grew apathetic and finally hostile. Repeatedly urging improvement in the curriculum, she cited as evidence the excellent work done by many very bright students in her freshman English classes.

Butler thought she was crazy; she simply didn't understand about "our special type of student." He used the fact that she thought her students bright as proof that she herself was stupid. Then, late in the first semester, an outside agency came in to administer a series of tests to the students to determine their effective reading levels and their functional school-grade level. When the results arrived in the dean's office shortly before Christmas, they showed that the college had several students reading and functioning at a school level as high as or higher than the grade in which they currently were enrolled. Many of them were freshmen, and most were in the English sections taught by Dr. Norden.

It was a revelation to the dean. Here he was worried about attracting a higher type of student to the campus, and lo and behold, some of them were already here. He reasoned that if he could do something special for these higher types they would not only stay at the college but also encourage their bright friends to come. It was an opportunity he could not well afford to miss. The upperclassmen, however, didn't seem worthy of his attention. Juniors and seniors were less likely to leave school before their graduation, and they were not apt to persuade their brighter friends to transfer to Thomas so late in the academic game. Butler would aim at the eight freshmen on the list. So, on the last day of the semester, he invited several "concerned parties" to his office to design an honors program for his eight higher-type freshmen, all of whom had been Dr. Norden's students. Butler summoned Mr. Geer from the reading laboratory, Miss Hobby from the speech laboratory, Mrs. Washington from the English department, and Dr. Harder, chairman of English and of the School of Arts and Letters. Dr. Norden was not invited.

I returned early from my Christmas holidays with the aim of sleeping late during the few remaining days of vacation, but I was awakened the first day by a call from the dean's secretary. It was absolutely essential, she said, that I come at once to Butler's office. I was still half asleep when I entered his office, and he began berating me for having left the campus two hours early before Christmas and thus missing one of the most important meetings of the year. He explained in detail the leave-of-absence forms I should have submitted, requesting to leave early, and the reasons why the administration would now find it necessary to deduct two hours' wages from my salary. But all this talk was only the customary preliminary browbeating procedure. Knowing it was actually the meeting I had missed that concerned him, I kept quiet and waited for him to arrive at the point. Neither of us mentioned that "one of the most important meetings of the year" had been called on one hour's notice on a day when most of the faculty had already left town; that, too, was customary procedure. Eventually he got around to telling me about the important meeting and its results. He spoke grandly of his plans to encourage our higher type of student and of the specific plan that had emerged from the pre-Christmas meeting. Each of the eight "higher-type" freshmen was to be enrolled in a "reading club"; membership entitled them to go to Mr. Geer's reading laboratory room at any time to read any of several novels he would keep for them in his office. Each student would be expected to read one book a week. Now what, Butler wanted to know, did I think of that?

The decision to have the reading club had already been reached by the group meeting, or at least the group had stamped its approval on Butler's plan, and Mr. Geer had agreed to take charge of distributing and collecting the books, making sure that no student took a book from the room and that each met his required book-per-week quota. But Butler would not be content with my saying simply that my opinion did not seem necessary when he had the unanimous decision of his committee before him. He was determined to have my approbation. I questioned him about

the purposes of the program and whether those purposes
would be met by a reading club, hoping that he might revise
his own thinking. But when he asked me point blank, "Do
you like the idea?" I had to say no.

He rolled out of his chair and loomed over the desk,
furious, demanding an explanation. I pointed out to him
that to require students to report to a particular room to
read an extra book per week under an instructor's eye was
to require more busywork from excellent students who already were discouraged by meaningless, time-consuming
assignments. It smacked of punishment rather than reward.
In the case of some of the students whom I knew personally,
to require supervised and selected reading of already avid
and wide-ranging readers was simply to insult their intelligence. And since no provisions had been made for selection
or discussion of the books, the students were going to receive their gold stars simply for plowing through the books
assigned; it didn't matter whether they understood them or
not, and certainly not whether they enjoyed them. Yet despite
my objections to the so-called Freshman Honors Program,
I had no hope of doing anything constructive on such short
notice. The dean wanted a program to begin with the new
semester—in about four days. A more efficient organization
might have devised a viable plan, but so little ever worked
out right at Thomas College that a sound program seemed
impossible. Still I started dreaming of my discussions with
Dr. Norden about provisions that might be made for these
good students: exemption from the deadening second semester of freshman English, with the freedom to choose another
course, to carry a reduced load and do their "own thing,"
or to pass on to a special honors section of sophomore literature, choosing their own books and perhaps their own instructor. I dreamed a little out loud, and in the next moment
Butler had picked up my dream and begun to run. I should
have known it would become a nightmare.

The reading club was discarded; the dean had a new plan. He personally would notify Chairman Harder and the eligible students that they were to be exempted from freshman English and assigned to my section of sophomore literature; my section would be limited to fifteen students so that I would have ample time to give the freshmen all the extra help they might need. I protested that his decision was being made unilaterally, arbitrarily; other faculty members might object; the committee would surely be insulted; there would be insurmountable conflicts in students' schedules; there was, in any case, no time to implement the plan and no assurance that it was worth anything anyway. But it was too late. His jaws were locked on what seemed to him a progressive idea and he was not about to let go. He pumped my hand, thanked me effusively for my cooperation and my wealth of good ideas, and assured me that he would "take care of everything." But I should have known better. Hadn't I just seen him completely reverse his field in the space of ten minutes?

A few days later, on the second day of registration for the new semester, the dean's officious secretary appeared with a list of eight names for Dr. Harder, ordering her to register these students in my sophomore literature section and giving her no explanation. Dr. Harder was understandably miffed that her Ph.D should be so little respected by a mere secretary, and she was soon buzzing with my colleagues. Meanwhile, some of the students on the list had already registered for the standard freshman courses and were nowhere to be found. Then three young men eligible for the program asked me if I knew what was going on; they had just run into the dean who told them that they were *required* to take my course but had not bothered to explain that they were being excused from freshman English. Upset at the thought of having to take two English courses, they had another problem as well. The dean had told them they must take my course, but it was being offered at the same time as a history course that they also were required to take now, according to the course instructor—the dean's wife.

In the midst of this confusion I was called away from Thomas by a family emergency. When I returned to campus, during the first week of classes, I learned that the three young men had chosen the history course and signed up for Mrs. Washington's sophomore literature; three girls had been advised by Dr. Harder to take her freshman English section under the mistaken notion that they would receive double credit; and another two girls had still not been informed of their privilege. The primary aim of putting the eight top-flight students in contact with one another had been defeated. In due time, the last two girls were informed of their option and entered my sophomore literature section, but they didn't learn very much because of the size of the class. During my absence from registration, the students had expressed their dislike for their former teachers by signing up with a new one—me; and the older teachers, enjoying the prospect of small sections and less work, had let them do it. As a result, they had ten or fifteen students in each of their sections, while my section, which was to have had fifteen to facilitate discussion among the eight "higher-type" freshmen, rounded off at fifty. Meanwhile, Dr. Norden, the best teacher in the department, had been denied further contact with the best students; she was assigned no sophomore courses.

I filed a written protest with the dean, complaining of the self-defeating implementation of the honors program and of the inequities in class loads, only to find myself the subject of a special departmental meeting called by an angry Butler. He denounced me for sabotaging the committee's reading club; my colleagues (except Dr. Norden) accused me of "coercing and enticing" their students away from them. And there was nothing I could say in my defense, for in a sense I had done the things of which I stood accused. I left the meeting longing to escape from the dean who had come full circle again and now found it safer to align himself with the old established retainers. Butler had his honors program on paper, where it would impress the accrediting officials and the higher types he wished to recruit for the student body; and he had achieved this triumph while demonstrating to the old guard that he was their strong ally. I had gained nothing but a reputation as everybody's enemy. I was shaken by the obvious fact that Butler had manipulated me in much the same way that he was being manipulated by Greeson. I would have to learn, as most of the students had, to keep my thoughts to myself and never, never try to change anything.

But the real losers were the so-called honor students. They had been pushed, pulled, ordered, commanded, and passed back and forth like so many field hands. Confused and upset, they went about the busywork of another ordinary class keeping their mouths shut and hoping everybody would soon forget that they were supposed to be smart.

The way I had been manipulated on this occasion was the way Butler was being manipulated all the time; it was what he was paid for. Gradually, he was losing himself in a maze of machinations, always bearing the responsibility and the blame for Greeson's plots and plans. By spring, he was a desperate man, searching for some thread that would make plain the pattern and the way out. He found it in "course outlines."

No one ever knew for certain where he got the idea, but he may have picked it up from the school contracts. For some arcane reason, each teacher was required in his official contract to "submit a course outline for each course taught." Just why this particular matter of routine should have appeared in the contract was a mystery, but its inclusion in that legal document lent it an air of majesty. In any case, the dean picked up the notion that educational activity was impossible without course outlines, and to that notion he clung with the tenacity of a drowning man. In committee meetings, faculty meetings, casual conversation, he some-how always railroaded the subject around to course outlines.

Late in the second semester, I was assigned to a committee on in-service training. The accrediting agency, after another inspection, had found several faculty members incompetent and many in need of additional training; the college, at the suggestion of the accrediting consultants, hoped to satisfy these deficiencies by an in-service training program, although it was clear from the outset that the administration did not know what an in-service training program was. They had apparently pondered the problem for several months with-out producing an answer; for with only three weeks remain-ing in the school year, Butler called together a faculty com-mittee to design an in-service training program to begin in August. Clearly it was to be another last-minute, slapdash, paper proposal in the grand tradition of the college. Butler's first question—"What do you think we ought to include in our in-service training program?"—let us know that he hadn't a clue. Committee members duly offered suggestions which the secretary duly noted; but for one reason or another Butler took exception to every recommendation. When we were exhausted, he "let us have [his] thinking on this matter of the utmost concern to all of us."

His thinking was course outlines. Each department was to assemble before the end of the term, and the members were to help each other draw up course outlines for fall semester courses. "Then," he announced, "in the fall you use your course outline to teach your course, and maybe you will find you want to make a little revision here and there, maybe you want to take this little part from here and put it over there, or maybe we won't have class on a Friday and you will have to do on Monday what you were supposed to do on Friday. That's all right. Unless you have to make too many changes or any big changes, in which would show you that you don't have a good outline and you aren't a good teacher. Then, after you teach the course in the fall, you will have all those little changes worked out and it will be just perfect for the next semester. Then when everyone is ready, the department chairman can have another meeting and you can help each other make outlines for another course and test that for one semester until you get it perfect."

By the dean's calculations, each teacher could "refine" one course each year. Since each teacher normally teaches four courses, at the end of four years he would have every course letter-perfect. Then the college would have perfect teachers teaching perfect courses, and the in-service training program could end. The success of the college would clearly be assured forevermore.

A few of the loyal retainers on the committee nodded approval, but most of us were too stunned to respond. His unreal and childlike plan was the epitome of all that Thomas College tended to: the triumph of form over substance. He had exposed his simple mind to us, and we sat in embarrassed silence.

The dumbfounded education chairman objected that he had never taught the same course twice in the same way, but the dean interrupted, "That's all right, Mr. Rogers. That's what we're here for—to help you. I'm sure that if we all work wholeheartedly on this program, we can all learn to teach our courses perfectly. The other members of your department will help you, Mr. Rogers. Don't worry."

Someone else suggested that we wouldn't know precisely what courses would be assigned us in the fall, but Butler brushed that off, too, as unimportant. "If you make a course outline for Course X and you are assigned to teach Course Y, you can just trade outlines with the person who made one for Course Y. You see, it's all very simple. I don't know what the problem is. It's all very simple."

We agreed. Our in-service training program had been designed for us. And it was all very simple.

By the time the dean submitted his annual request for

federal aid to the Department of Health, Education, and Welfare, he had a full report from his in-service training committee to include in the college's proposal. Under the impressive heading "Advancing Education in the Seventies," the committee report stated: "It is appropriate that research on course outlines be prosecuted because this matter is of significance to faculty and students in pursuing the instructional programs of the college." The "problem and objective" of this aspect of the in-service training program, the committee said, was "to investigate the most productive ways and means for the formulation and utilization of outlines." The major objective—among many listed for the program— was "to challenge the instructional staff to produce increased cognizance of the scope, methodology, and appropriateness of courses." The methods used to achieve this grand objective would undoubtedly be much like the method of the initial meeting: the faculty would listen to Butler's "thinking."

The report had to look good on paper, however, so the committee produced a list of official "implementations":

1. Hold investigatory meeting to determine the locus of responsibilities for the formulation of outlines, whether with the various schools, the departments, or with individual faculty members; to probe, also, other relevant issues.

2. During first semester, ascertain the effectiveness of course outlines by conducting a student poll.

3. Ascertain the effectiveness of newly devised course outlines during the second semester by conducting a student poll and comparing effectiveness with the first poll.

4. Probe problems concerning the fundamental forms and sections of a course outline with the assistance of a consultant at a general meeting of the entire instructional staff held for this purpose. At this meeting a compilation of course outlines in all academic fields from other colleges would be on view.

To make the in-service training program appear thoroughly modern and up-to-date, the report also called for the development of "team teaching," which it termed "a radical departure . . . from the traditional." The main chore of team teachers, however, like that of every other instructor, was to "meet to plan to form an outline [of] their course."

To implement this program, the college asked the federal government for $16,400 annually for three years. Forty-nine thousand dollars may seem a high price to pay for course outlines, but part of the sum designated for in-service training was to be used not for the teachers' outlines but for a vaguely defined program of in-service training for the college maintenance men.

In his request to the federal government, Dean Butler had to admit that the older instructors were "resistant to . . . revising course outlines and experimenting with team-teaching." Nevertheless, the dean concluded confidently, "We have formulated an effective In-Service Program. . . . Instruction has advanced in all academic areas of the College; . . . course outlines have advanced." The success of the program was clearly a measure of the dean's leadership.

The dean had begun his term of office with elaborate plans for the wholesale revision of the college; after a year of his administration it would be a brave new institution. The college would be accredited, and the dean's favors would be sought by established and respected schools; maybe he would even become part of the "black brain-drain," taking an excellent administrative position at a Northern white university—with, of course, a fabulous salary into the bargain. But it hadn't worked out that way. During the second semester he spent much of his time calling faculty members to his office to discuss their course outlines. He was dissatisfied with my sophomore literature course outline because it simply listed the books in the order in which they were to be read; it was an outline much like those I had been given as a student at a major university. He needed an exact timetable and a clear statement of what was to be said about each book: names, dates, facts, figures. But by that time, I had learned a few tricks myself. This semester, I told him, I was taking notes on everything I said in class; by the end of the term I would be able to give him a detailed outline of everything I would say in class next year together with the dates on which I would say it. He was pleased.

By the end of the year we would see him lurking behind a door or in the shadow at the end of a corridor in the classroom building. He was checking to see that the teachers came to class on time.

Everything the dean did played into Greeson's hands. Even when Butler, for a series of capricious reasons—many of them having to do with course outlines—fired almost half the faculty, it was still all right with President Greeson. When he took office, Greeson reportedly made a rash promise to the board of trustees that he would gain accreditation for the college or resign. He had now held office for several years, and the college was not yet accredited or likely to be. But the most hardheaded trustee would have to sympathize with the problems presented to a president by such a dean. Butler didn't know it, but he was acting his assigned role perfectly.

Part of the dean's success in camouflaging Greeson's tyranny from faculty and students was the result of his ambitious efforts to establish a tyranny of his own. He became—in more than one sense—king of a paper empire. Conservationists on the faculty lamented the forests that must have been decimated to provide material for Butler's favorite weapon—the memo. Without Butler, the faculty mailboxes might have yawned empty for weeks at a time, but the busy dean stuffed them every day with memos and notices of the important and the trivial. He had a preternatural gift for getting out the premature announcement. At noon, when most faculty members picked up their mail, on the way to the cafeteria, one would find a series of notices, all bearing that day's date. "This is to inform you that the prior scheduled meeting has been changed to an hour later in the Science building." "This is to inform you that the meeting announced before will be rescheduled." "This is to inform you that the rescheduled meeting will be scheduled for two hours earlier on the date in question in the Arts and Letters building." There might be three or four such notices, all put in the mailboxes during a single morning, with no indication of the sequence in which they had been written. The instructors would spread them out on their lunch tables, juggling them in a hopeless effort to find some coherent sequence; but each order made just as much sense as any other order. And none of the memos was particularly informative anyway; there were so many meetings that one never knew which meeting was being referred to. And if one were canny enough to figure out which meeting was to be held at what hour, he still faced the task of searching through all the rooms of the Science building or the Arts and Letters building to find which room was to be used for the gathering. Sometimes committee meetings turned into ludicrous games of musical chairs, with eight or ten members wandering the halls looking for the unspecified meeting room and for each other. If they happened to meet, they would band together to search for the chairman; but there were cases where the committee and the chairman never found each other.

Nevertheless, Butler's rule became: Put it in writing. That, of course, is not a bad idea, assuming that one can write intelligible English. Unfortunately, the rhetorical idiosyncrasies of Greeson, Butler, and the older faculty members appeared on paper like a kind of baroque code. Butler's addition of supposedly businesslike phrases—such as *in re* and *to wit* didn't clarify much. He would send out notices reading: "This is to inform you that the library has sent to each faculty member a list in re periodicals to wit check in which ones the library should continue to describe and in which should be continued." If an instructor failed to act on those instructions he, and every other instructor, would receive a second notice a few weeks later: "In re library periodicals: This is to inform you that you are the only faculty member who has not submitted the necessary required information in which was required."

Such memos from Butler were difficult to decipher, but not impossible, once you got the hang of it. Harder to deal with were the notices that transferred to paper the prevalent verbal habit of not saying what one meant, nor meaning what one said. Take, for example, a memo that read: "This is to inform you that the consultants from the University in re consulting will be on the campus tomorrow." That might be only a simple bit of information. Or, one might learn later, when called on the carpet to explain his absence, that the notice constituted an instruction to attend an important meeting at 4:00 P.M. in room 408 of the Arts and Letters building. One could try to explain, but Butler would counter: "The fact remains that I sent you a memo in which this meeting was, and you didn't come to the meeting. That is dereliction of duty."

Butler's habit of commanding rather than informing also contributed to the chaotic situation. When Dr. Norden and I received memos ordering us to report to the maintenance shed at six o'clock the next morning, we thought that Butler had finally gone berserk, until it occurred to us that one of our colleagues was having a little joke at the dean's expense. But we learned the next day, while being sternly reprimanded by Butler, that had we complied with his instructions we and the other members of the department would have been driven to a leading university for a tour and consultation with its English department faculty. The senior members of our department, trained to obey the most insane commands without question, had duly appeared at the shed and been transported to the university. But in any case, there was no way that Dr. Norden and I could have performed what was expected of us. Had we followed orders, we would have reported to the shed at six, found no one there, and returned home. Our colleagues and their driver, however, knew that six o'clock did not mean six o'clock. They all reported promptly at the time *really* intended: six-thirty.

The memo system was hopeless, but it padded everybody's files and fostered the appearance of a busy and businesslike establishment. When memos failed, however, the dean had another weapon: the committee.

Committees at Thomas are an effective administrative tool, not for any of the reasons one might suppose, but simply because they produce the illusion of democratic process. At Thomas, all the standing committees were created by the president; he appointed all the members and named the chairmen. Thus, each committee could be effectively weighted in favor of the old guard; the results of any votes the committees might cast were clear from the moment their composition was announced in a presidential memo. Moreover, by carefully defining the province of each committee, Greeson established certain aspects of college life as proper for discussion, while keeping touchy aspects safely out of bounds. There was a homecoming committee to plan what should have been a student activity, there was a friendship committee to send flowers to the temporarily incapacitated, but there was no committee on student or faculty affairs.

There was, however, a Committee on Standards and Instructional Programs, the most important campus committee and the only one that held meetings on something like a regular basis. Its province was the curriculum. Through this committee passed all proposals to alter in any way the present curricula or degree requirements. Its potential for improving the college was enormous. But it was chaired by Dean Butler.

The committee operated according to Butler's rules—or whims. Rule 1 was that any proposal to be brought before the committee must be in Butler's hands a week before the meeting. There is nothing wrong with that rule; in fact, it is usually standard committee procedure that proposals be made available to all members for study before a meeting. Butler's rule, however, was designed not to facilitate discussion and prompt action but to give him time to receive his orders from Greeson; for the fate of a proposal depended not upon the committee, but upon the president. When Butler had orders to pass a proposal, it could be introduced without prior notice; he might even introduce it himself, cutting off discussion and calling for an immediate affirmative vote on the grounds that the measure was "urgent and essential." A committee member who asked for discussion or voted "nay" might become the victim of one of Butler's raving personal attacks. Proposals passed in this cursory fashion proceeded directly to Greeson for his immediate implementation.

Proposals that were not supposed to pass had a harder time. They might be sent back for approval by the concerned department or school or both. Butler might claim that the wording was ambiguous and return a proposal for rewriting. He might simply throw a proposal away, refusing even to discuss it on the grounds that the budget was insufficient or that the accreditation board wouldn't approve. If an unwelcome proposition was scheduled to come to a vote despite his best efforts, he could stack the meeting with his minions simply by failing to notify recalcitrant members of the meeting. And if all else failed, he could blow up and stomp out of the room, declaring as he departed that the meeting had not been "official" anyway.

To the harried members of the committee, the difference between the two kinds of proposal was clear. Anything that looked good on paper but required no real change in procedure was to pass. Any measure that would significantly update or upgrade curricula, lighten the load of busywork on the students, or subtly shift the balance of power was to be defeated. If, by some fluke, a measure that was supposed to fail passed, it then had to go to the entire faculty for a confirming vote before it could be submitted to the president. At full faculty meetings, Greeson himself took charge, and his methods, although more subtle, were no different in kind from Butler's. Someone once suggested to Butler that meetings be conducted according to Robert's Rules of Order. He replied, quite correctly, that "what is good for Robert may not be good for Thomas."

The other standing committees of the college met seldom, if at all. The chairmen received their orders from Greeson or Butler and carried them out. Like Butler, a few of the chairmen liked to go through the motions of holding rubber-stamp meetings, but most didn't enjoy that tedious process and didn't bother with it. When one of the accreditation board consultants asked to see the dean's files of minutes of the standing committees, however, the directive went out to chairmen to submit the minutes of each meeting. Immediately, every committee met so the chairmen could record some minutes to send in, but it was clear at those meetings that there really was nothing to discuss, no reason for getting together. There were few meetings after that. Instead, we occasionally found in our mailboxes the minutes of meetings that had never been held, and we read with fascination of the things we had said and the votes we had cast in support of the administration.

There were other temporary committees, too, like the dean's honors program committee: groups of people summoned to Butler's office on a moment's notice to nod approval of his latest program. Nobody liked to be named to one of the dean's temporary committees because it always involved doing some work; one might be "asked" to help clean the library or to alphabetize the index of the latest report to the accreditation board. Service on Butler's committees wasn't very stimulating, but it was, as the dean so often said, urgent and essential. Yet everyone must have suspected that all the phony committees, the fake minutes, and the profusion of verbose memos were designed only to make the underlings feel that they were involved in "the action."

The action, however, was not in Butler's office. Nor was it in Greeson's. For just as Greeson used Butler as a tool and a façade, he was himself being used by a more powerful administrator: the vice-president, who was in charge of business affairs. Apparently, the only significant difference between Butler and Greeson was that Greeson had more leverage and more smarts. As a result, Greeson grew rich while Butler grew frantic. Richer still was the man with the cash register and the brick doghouse, the vice-president.

Mr. Baggett was a tall, lean, hungry-looking man, a sort of swarthy Abe Lincoln, but instead of a beard he sported a tiny, paintbrush mustache. From his small, musty office in the administration building, he presided over all the operations of the business office. And although his office was crammed with unnecessary employees, each occupying an important niche on the management flow chart, his was for all practical purposes a one-man operation. He directed the entire budget of the school.

The college received its funds from several sources. Its main support was the federal government, but federal funds arrived in many packages: general grants, building grants, special project grants, work-study grants, loans for which the individual students had contracted with the government under the National Defense Education Act, and an occasional pork-barrel kickback from a racist congressman who wanted to be sure the "nigras" would stay in their own school. A religious denomination with which the college officially was associated sent a little money. Bigger grants came from Ford and other educational foundations. The school cafeteria, bookstore, and laundry all operated at a tidy profit. There were some state funds and state scholarship monies and a few contributions from local industry and alumni. A little money came in tuition fees and more from the Veteran's Administration for GI Bill students. Many of the funds received had strings attached—they were earmarked for specific projects or specific students.

The college's official reports leave the exact amount and sources of its income a mystery, for the figures disagree from year to year and often from page to page. One college report to the Department of Health, Education, and Welfare, credits the National Defense Student Loan Program, administered by HEW, with a contribution of $173,000 for 1970; another gives the figure as $198,500. More confusing than the obvious discrepancies, however, is the misleading form of the college budget, a form required by HEW. Since many state and federal programs provide money to individual students rather than to the institution, the college budget presents its students as the source of income that is actually derived from government. Such individual contracts between the student and the government are managed by the college; the student himself never sees the money, although he usually is obligated to pay it back to the government in hard cash. The arrangement enables many needy students to attend college, but it also produces some wildly misleading figures in the institutional budget. Thomas reports that in 1970 it collected $529,000 in tuition and fees (more than $1,000 from each student) and earned $260,000 from the operation of "auxiliary enterprises," presumably the student cafeteria, laundry, and school store. The federal government is listed as contributing only $100,000 for "sponsored research" (whatever that may be), the state government as

contributing nothing. Another report, however, acknowl-
edges that 98 per cent of the students were receiving financial
aid in 1970. Still another report puts the figure at 100 per
cent of the students receiving 90 per cent support. That
support came from an Educational Opportunity grant of
$203,900, National Defense student loans of $198,500 (elsewhere given as $173,000), a college work-study program of
$191,600—all from HEW—and state student-aid funds of
$178,000. Added up, the aid to students from state and fed-
eral governments comes to $772,000, a figure that closely ap-
proximates the college's reported income of $789,000 from
tuition, fees, and auxiliary enterprises. Almost all of the
school's income, then, comes from government, but when
the indebtedness belongs officially to the students rather than
to the institution, the temptation must be strong to charge
the student whatever the traffic in government funds will
bear. Strangely enough, the college lists on its budget under
the heading "Student aid income for scholarships, fellowships, prizes" only one figure: zero.

"Cooperative programs"—in which HEW pays Thomas to
employ consultants from other colleges to improve its own
programs—brought Thomas $42,284 in 1970: $28,061 to
cooperate with one university in strengthening the speech and
reading laboratories at Thomas, $8,402 to cooperate with an-
other in reviving the faculty, and $5,821 to cooperate with a
third in upgrading teacher education. HEW also granted
$8,000 for faculty fellowships to permit at least one professor
to return to graduate school for additional study. In a further
effort to improve the faculty, HEW gave the college $20,000
in 1970 to attract two visiting scholars and $13,800 to pay
two national teaching fellows, all of whom were to be recruited and hired by the school. Then there was a $16,000
supplemental grant from HEW, a $2,500 grant from the Ford
Foundation, and another small grant from another foundation to pay for faculty travel to academic conferences; a

grant of $100,000 shared with five other colleges in a state-wide consortium; another HEW Title III grant of $15,821 for "business administration and student services," an HEW Title VE grant of $3,333 for an administrators' workshop; and another $25,000 for another workshop. For 1970, the college also lists $24,500 in endowment earnings, $17,000 from "other sources," and the astonishing figure—which it was not required to break down—of $281,000 in "private gifts and grants." It must have been difficult to keep such a complicated budget straight.

Of course, the federal government is supposed to check up on how the taxpayers' money is spent. The federal funds Thomas receives come from the Division of College Support of the Bureau of Higher Education, a department of the U.S. Office of Education, which itself is a branch of the Department of Health, Education, and Welfare. The Division of College Support is charged with auditing at least once every three years the books of every college receiving its aid. Auditing the books of a college, however, is a big job; and the division is understaffed. When an audit is made, it sometimes results in indictments of college administrators; and the division has closed more than one college. But if it has performed such an audit of the Thomas account—the college has received federal aid under Title III since 1967—I was not allowed to see the records.

As an additional check, the division also sends its officers on periodic inspection trips of the colleges receiving aid. Such inspections often produce evidence that immediate changes must be made, and the inspector may find himself increasingly involved with two or three schools requiring drastic change. Inspection of the other colleges in his file must be postponed until the next year, or perhaps the year after that. So it is with the officer responsible for Thomas College. By his own account, he has performed wonders, transforming several small colleges into genuine educational

institutions at the rate of approximately two each year. Unfortunately, he bears the responsibility for over 300 such
colleges, and when Thomas was granted aid for the fifth con-
secutive year, he still had never visited its campus or met its
administrators. He knew of Thomas only what the college
had told him in its annual reports, and he hadn't even had
time to read those carefully. He had not noticed the frequent discrepancies from one year to the next in the figures
provided by the college. Nor had he noticed that the glowing
progress report most recently received from Dean Butler had
been copied, almost verbatim, from the report of a previous
dean submitted a few years earlier. When I pointed out
some of these odd items to the officer during an interview,
he agreed that "someone ought to look into that."

Naturally, at the end of each fiscal year, Thomas comes
out in or near the red. The federal government increases
its grants each year, but somehow there is never quite enough
money to go around. At least that is what Mr. Baggett says,
and he is probably the only man who knows just how much
money comes into the college and how much goes out. Yet
while the college staggers along, Mr. Baggett seems to be
thriving.

Baggett's authority in all matters affecting business affairs
is beyond challenge. And almost all matters, in one way or
another, are tied to business affairs. His power was made
painfully clear to the faculty during a rather mild reformist
move to improve the school bookstore. Faculty members
were required to order textbooks for their classes through
the school store. If and when the books arrived, many of
them were sold to the students at inflated prices, the cost
appearing on their monthly bill, which was then charged off
against their NDEA loan account. The difference between
the cost of a book to the school and the subsequent cost to
the student must have been substantial, but no one knew

where the money went. No one seemed to notice that the students were being cheated, but several instructors were upset when their textbooks did not arrive.

The bookstore was "supervised" by an old friend of Mr. Baggett's who was kept on the pay roll for the sole purpose of ordering textbooks. He did a little work in the fall, a little in the spring, but mostly he lounged in his private office, smoking one cigar after another. Baggett's generous provision for his friend probably would have passed unremarked if only Mr. Tilly had known how to order books. It seemed a simple enough job. Mr. Tilly, however, ordered all books from the state schoolbook warehouse, the graveyard for obsolete textbooks, on the mistaken notion that it was the original source of all books published in the United States. If the warehouse didn't have a book, Mr. Tilly would inform you—when you went to him to trace your book order—that no such book had ever been published. Mr. Tilly's ordering system had caused no problems for the older faculty members, who for years had been teaching classes from old textbooks retired by state high schools, but new, young instructors, wishing to use current texts and paperbacks, were appalled.

I was among them. After weeks of waiting for a particular paperback to arrive, I went to Mr. Tilly only to be informed that there was no such book. When his system became clear to me, I tried vainly to explain the difference between a publishing house and a textbook warehouse. There were a few books, I told him, published outside of the state. Flabbergasted, he refused to believe it.

"Don't take my word for it, Mr. Tilly. You write to this address in New York City and I'll be willing to bet a day's pay that they'll send you the books."

But he would have none of it. Like many Americans, he was distrustful of New York. If he sent a letter to New York, there was no telling what might come back through the mail: Communist literature, marijuana, a bomb. So I gave up and wrote to the publisher myself. Within a week, I was called to the business office; my books had arrived.

"But," Mr. Tilly said, "all book orders have to be made by me and have to have Mr. Baggett's approval. So we sent your books back to New York."

When I calmed down, I wrote a letter to the president and the dean informing them of the situation and expressing my deep regret that, owing to the lack of textbooks, I would be unable to fulfill the purposes of my course as presented in my course outline. Several young faculty members had suffered similar experiences, and they too filed protests with Greeson and Butler. Soon we received a memo announcing a special faculty meeting for the purpose of discussing improvement of the bookstore. We were all elated, but our joy was smothered quickly under a long presidential address on the general topic of friendly cooperation. Greeson's folksy speech was followed by an hour-long lecture from a belligerent Mr. Baggett on how to fill out the book-order forms, allowing ninety days for delivery. There was no discussion.

Fortunately, Mr. Tilly took it upon himself to improve. He "asked around" and discovered that there were indeed some books published outside of the state, some even in New York. After that he was willing to send orders to the addresses we gave him, and eventually we received most of the texts we wanted. But we had all learned that we could not question Mr. Baggett's rule; Greeson would always follow his orders—even if it meant that the students had to go without books.

So far as anyone knew, in all Baggett's years at the college, there had been only one real challenge to his power. Years before, after a disastrous series of one-year presidents, the trustees had brought in a young, dynamic black minister from a large Northern city to restore order. President Stout was a reformer and a man of action; in a single year he had overhauled the faculty and the curriculum. The faculty, at least the younger teachers, admired and respected him; the students adored him. Then he tackled the college bureaucracy. Heads rolled. He fired several members of the vice-president's staff and cut into the administrative bureaucracy, firing another of Baggett's friends, the dean of student affairs, who, at that time, was Simon L. Greeson. Then, coming prematurely to the inevitable power struggle, he fired Mr. Baggett. It was all very quiet; many didn't know that it had happened. So it came to most people as a surprise when, a few days later, the bishop of the church, head of the board of trustees, announced the resignation of President Stout. Mr. Baggett returned to his office; a nondescript fellow filled in as president for a year or two; and then Simon Greeson returned to move into the big house.

Thomas College, then, it should be clear, was no community of scholars; rather, it was a clearly defined but carefully disguised pecking order. Baggett used Greeson who used Butler who used the faculty who used the students. The curious way in which all ranks in the pecking order unwittingly conspired to keep the henhouse roof from falling in is perhaps best illustrated by a case history. It might be called: The Case of the Dummy Professor.

During my first semester at Thomas, I was assigned to teach the two sections of remedial English. The course was listed in the catalogue as English 0, "a course in the fundamentals of speaking and writing English," but the faculty referred to it as "Zero English" and the students called it "dummy class." The kids assigned to the class were deeply resentful of being more or less officially classified as dummies, particularly at a small school where everyone knew who the members of the dummy class were. And they resented having to attend class five hours each week while receiving no academic credit for their work. A few students withdrew from the school rather than take the course. One of the young men assigned to Zero English—a dummy who officially was supposed to be incapable of expressing himself— angrily wrote a composition on the subject.

> I think all o courses should be dropped because they are no help toward your education. While you are taking the o courses and getting no credit for them, you could be getting credit for the main courses. In the o course we are taught the same thing as the [main] course, and why shouldn't we get the same credit hours?
>
> Just because we have fail to score high enough on a place-ment test we are said to be the slow students. When you pay your money you don't give a dam about your slowness; you just want to get what you pay for. I know that you don't want to pay for anything that you don't need.
>
> I don't think this is fair to us as students. Now can you tell me why or if you should take o courses? You can't find a reasonable answer. It is too late to help ourselves, but we could help others if we got o courses from the curriculum of [Thomas] College.

Many other students simply gave up on English; if they were to be called dummies anyway, they might as well act the part. Their case was, as Charles E. Silberman explains it in discussing the poor reading ability of so many "dis-advantaged" youngsters:

> . . . the principal way in which people develop a sense of ego, of self-knowledge and self-confidence, is by developing com-petence in first one area and then in others. When failure has been repeated frequently enough, it is almost inevitable that the child will begin to hate himself—and to hate school and the teachers which make public the evidence of his failure. And then the vicious circle begins. Because the child cannot read, his attitude suffers; he may simply withdraw from com-petition, to persuade himself that he really could have passed if only he had tried; or he may become a clown or a rebel. . . . The combination of inadequate . . . skill and poor attitude reinforces the failure, which reinforces the attitude. And so it goes.[1]

[1] Charles E. Silberman, *Crisis in Black and White* (New York: Random House, 1964), pp. 268–69.

Dummy class presented the perfect setting for the vicious circle Silberman describes. Each morning I faced students divided more or less equally into three groups: the clowns and cut-ups, determined to prevent work; the smolderingly hostile, determined not to do any work anyway; and the abjectly defeated, convinced that they couldn't work if they tried and dedicated instead to daydreaming and sleeping. The classes presented what teachers given to euphemism call a "challenge."

The course was supposed to consist of a review of basic grammar through the practice of diagraming sentences. According to Dr. Harder, the English chairman, I was to lead my reluctant charges through the whole bag of grammatical tricks once again—from conjunctions to adverbial clauses. It was a dismal prospect. In the first place, there are volumes of educational research demonstrating that there is no positive correlation between a student's ability to solve objective grammar problems and his ability to write what he has to say in clear and precise English; and I knew from my own years of teaching that the best scores on objective grammar tests are often made by foreign students who can't put together an idiomatic English sentence but have no trouble memorizing lists of irregular verb forms and possessive pronouns. There are even more volumes of research— based upon classroom experience and recent linguistic studies—suggesting countless better ways of grappling with the problem of teaching basic writing and speaking. Besides, my students had already demonstrated in high school their inability to master sentence diagraming. There seemed little point in repeating that "required" but meaningless activity. Consequently, I quietly began using methods and projects like those I was using with my regular freshman English class, and I perceived immediately that there was only one significant difference between my regular students and my dummies: the dummies responded more quickly and with greater enthusiasm to being treated, for a change, like normal, responsible adults.

· The freshmen had been assigned to the two groups on the basis of their scores on a standardized English placement test. Observing that there apparently was no correlation between test score and class performance, I investigated the testing procedure. The highest possible score on the test was 60, but the top performance by a Thomas freshman was 21, with most of the scores falling below 16. For placement purposes, however, anything above 10 was considered normal; anything below, substandard. The figure was a purely arbitrary one chosen by Dr. Harder, presumably because it was a nice round number. To discriminate two groups of students from such a small range of scores seemed ridiculous.

Although I thought I could present a good case against Zero English on the basis of the test scores and my classroom experience, I decided to take the placement test myself to see what the students were up against. The test itself, I found, was ludicrous. It consisted of a series of readings with small portions of several sentences underlined in each reading passage. Corresponding with each underlined portion were three alternative versions of that bit of the sentence. The student was to mark on his answer sheet the best of the four versions, the original wording and punctuation or one of the three alternatives. The test, however, was not on correct grammar and punctuation, but rather on preferred usage. Of the four versions given for a sentence bit, two or even three of them might be technically correct; the real problem was to choose the "most correct" of two or three correct possibilities. That choice, of course, is largely a matter of personal taste—the taste of the man who engineered the test. By the time I was halfway through the test, I found myself in complete disagreement with the tester's rather old-fashioned preferences, although I could easily guess what his preferences would be. I began responding to the man who was administering my test by saying, "I prefer B, but the right answer will be C"; and I left him amazed at my psychic powers.

The black counselor giving me the test had also administered it to the freshmen, and he told me a "sad" story about "just how dumb some of them really are." Several students, he said, had looked over the test and promptly fallen asleep. Glancing back over the test readings, I thought I knew why. The first story was about spring housecleaning; after father had left for the office, mother carefully wrapped the dining-room chandelier in linen and rolled up the oriental carpet. Then she set to work cleaning everything in the room, including the silver and crystal. It was a nice little story, full of wholesome American virtue, but it was not the kind of story that a kid from the back streets of Memphis or a dirt farm in the Delta can grow very excited about.

The use of this test to place Thomas students was a perfect example of the widespread misuse of standardized tests denounced by more insightful educators.

> The introduction and misapplication of the whole system of educational testing in the traditional Negro college best illustrates the inappropriate use of an educational device that has done irreparable harm to countless thousands of black American students. So-called national standardized tests reflect a basic cultural bias in favor of nonblack middle-class values and certainly do not constitute an accurate or fair gauge of the environment and experiences of black life in the United States.[2]

I began to understand the plaintive paper I had received from a young woman in dummy class after I asked the students to write down some items they would like to study.

> My most favorite subject has always been English. What I had to study didn't matter because I would always enjoy getting it.

---

[2] Tilden J. LeMelle and Wilbert J. LeMelle, *The Black College: A Strategy for Achieving Relevancy* (New York: Praeger, 1969), p. 26.

You have ask your class to name things they would like to do and I really think it's great, but having never had this opportunity before makes me feel different toward English. I think it would be great if you would start off, and then maybe I can understand your method of teaching English or learn what's most important as a college student.

Public speaking, reciting poems, acting in plays, and reading stories is really what I'm engrossed in. But then there have been many times when I was told to read a certain article and from that day to this one didn't get a clear understanding. I worry about things of this sort.

It is said I fail the placement test, but that was all I was told. Some of the English I had never seen anything like it before so all I could do at that time was what I thought was best.

Whatever you teach in this class is fine with me, but I do wish you could get me one of those placement tests and explain some of that English if you think it's necessary.

With my ammunition in hand, I spoke to the president about the injustice of Zero English. To my surprise, he agreed wholeheartedly with my view that the course should be dropped from the curriculum; he even encouraged me to initiate action "through the proper channels" to do away with the course. Meanwhile, some of my dummies, on their own initiative, had gone to the president with their complaints about the course. Greeson, they said, had been very sympathetic. One student reported to me in a composition: "The President of the College spoke against having a o course in English. I went and talk to him about it, and he said he was going to try to do something about it." For years, President Greeson claimed, he had wanted to discontinue the course, but his hands were tied. Now, he assured the students, their instructor would take the necessary steps. In the meantime, they would just have to bear with the present situation.

With this assurance, I prepared a detailed proposal calling for an end to Zero English and the placement of all freshmen in sections of the regular freshman English course, sections small enough so that all students could receive individual help. Early in October, I submitted the proposal to the English department, where it passed over the opposition of Chairman Harder, who habitually thought and acted as though all Thomas students were dummies. The following week, I brought the proposal before the School of Arts and Letters, where it passed again over the opposition of Chairman Harder. Next the proposal went to the dean's Committee on Standards and Instructional Programs, but I was not invited to appear before the group; Dr. Harder, who did not understand the proposal, presented her own version. The result was hopeless confusion and a decision from the dean to throw out the whole idea. Several sympathetic committee members, however, led by Dr. Norden and Mr. Rogers, passed a motion instructing Butler to invite me to the next meeting, when the proposal would be reconsidered.

Knowing of this transaction, I waited for my invitation from Butler. It didn't come. With my suspicions aroused, I realized that all the opposition to my rather innocent little proposal was coming from above. Dr. Harder had opposed it at two meetings and had done her best to sabotage it at a third. The dean clearly was ready to throw it out altogether. Yet I knew President Greeson to be in favor of my plan. The pieces didn't fit. Without invitation, I went to the next instructional programs committee meeting to search for a clue.

Butler seemed a little shaken by my entrance, but it left him no choice but to discuss my proposal. At first, the discussion went smoothly, but when it appeared that I was winning over the committee, Butler pounced. He had an objection to every point I raised, but as sympathy increased, his objections became more and more obviously farfetched. Committee members repeatedly announced that they were ready to vote, but Butler refused to close discussion: he had more objections to make. Suddenly, after an hour, he crumbled. Slumping in his seat, he called for a vote, and with only Dr. Harder in opposition, the proposal passed.

The committee members believed that the terms of the proposal could take effect immediately, and since it was then only the middle of November, they saw no reason why my zero classes couldn't be immediately retitled so that my dummies could gain academic credit for the current semester's work and become eligible for the regular second-semester English course. Butler, however, announced a new rule: All proposals passing the instructional programs committee must be approved by the full faculty before they can take effect. In private, though, he assured me that my proposal would come before the full faculty as soon as possible, certainly before the end of the semester. He, too, he said, was in full sympathy with my proposal; his objections at the committee meeting had been only appropriate to his position as devil's advocate.

Unconvinced and uneasy, I waited, bolstered a little by support from an unexpected quarter. One of the senior members of the social studies faculty, a black woman whom I scarcely knew, sent me a personal note.

> I wish to express my appreciation to you for the interest you have shown the students in regard to zero English.
> I have known students to express utter disgust for the course. A few years ago one student had to repeat it, and she finally withdrew. I have long felt that it shouldn't take forever for one to realize how damaging an experience can be to the student. From the outside one hesitates to be critical, but I thank God for your insight.

Grateful as I was for my colleague's letter, I thought it rather odd that instead of sending it through the inter-campus mail she had delivered it personally to my house one evening, nervously declining my offer of coffee, darting back into the dark as quickly as she had come. I was too stupid to understand that with her years of experience at

Thomas, she knew the administration much better than I did.

Meetings of the full faculty were frequent, but my proposal never appeared on the agenda, and new business could not be brought up from the floor. "How does one get an item of business on the agenda?" I asked Butler. The agenda was prepared, he told me, by President Greeson, who "knows best" what is important. After all, we couldn't discuss everything at once, could we?

The semester passed and so did my dummies, with colors flying but still dissatisfied and resentful. They had begun to think that I, too, had betrayed their confidence. As the new semester approached, I discovered that Dr. Harder had assigned me to teach two more sections of dummies. She anticipated several dummies among the transfer students who would enroll at midyear; and she firmly expected that, as in previous years, most of my first-semester dummies would flunk. When at registration time she didn't have enough official dummies on hand to make up even one section, she was furious. I had certified two whole sections of idiots as reasonably competent in their native language; clearly, I had betrayed Dr. Harder's principles. My superiors and colleagues now had good grounds for questioning my professional training, my ethics, and my intelligence.

Finally, in the middle of April, several proposals passed by the instructional programs committee came before the full faculty for approval; mine was among them. Butler presided, but Greeson sat among the faculty, seizing the floor when he needed it to make sure the proceedings developed as he desired. Thinking that Greeson supported my proposal, I was stunned when he raised the first objection.

"This plan doesn't seem to meet the needs in which our special type of student has. It sounds all right, but you all know that as I have said many times before and will say again we must make progress in which includes the special needs of our special type of student."

But I had learned by this time to roll with the punch. I countered that provision had been made in the program for special tutorial services. To his every objection, I had an answer; and several faculty members bravely spoke in favor of the proposal. Greeson, however, had voiced his opposition plainly, and Butler called for a vote.

"All those in favor," he said, and hands went up all over the room. Hands still upraised, we peeked furtively at each other with nervous smiles, like guilty children caught in the act of doing something inescapably naughty but ever so much fun. It was the only time during the year that I saw anything go against Greeson's wishes.

The fun was short-lived, however, for Butler announced at the close of the meeting that all the proposals passed by the faculty would now be sent to Greeson for his approval. They were, he said, only "recommendations." I inquired whether there was any established procedure for the president to report back to the faculty on his action. There was no established procedure. It would be unnecessary, anyway, Butler said, because President Greeson was "a man of honor." That, of course, was the last anyone heard of my proposal.

I understood that I had been manipulated and used again. Greeson had given me the go-ahead, then dispatched Butler to throw up a roadblock. Butler, in turn, had put Dr. Harder in my path and, later, his instructional programs committee. At some point in the "proper channels," my proposal was destined to crash. But in the meantime, my activity proved highly useful; it kept me diverted from other games in which, I still fondly believed, I might have inflicted real damage to the old guard. And, more important, it was used by Greeson and Butler and unwittingly by me to keep the dummies hopeful and docile. We had all played the game very well, each with our own proper cards, all helping to keep the house in business. It was simply a series of freakish moves that had carried the proposal through and forced Greeson himself out of hiding to smash it.

But there was still one piece that didn't fit. What was behind Greeson's opposition? What was so important to him that he was willing to expose himself as a dictator in destroying the proposal himself?

The answer, of course, was money. The college knew that the U.S. Office of Education looks with favor on remedial and developmental programs, and that under Title III of the Higher Education Act of 1965 it has a lot of money to dispense for such programs. Since 1967, Thomas had received federal money for its reading and speech laboratories, known officially as the Communications Skills Center, and the amount of the grant had been increased each year. To keep the money coming in, the college had to emphasize the inadequate preparation of its students and the continued need for operation of the center. The center *was* needed, but it was needed by almost all the students, not by just a few dummies. At times, the college seemed to recognize that fact. A recent report to the Division of College Support of HEW asserted, "Of 542 students enrolled this semester . . . 451 attend classes at the Center." Unfortunately, this figure is probably far from accurate since only some freshmen are required to attend classes at the center, and the center itself, which sounds so impressive on paper, consists of two teachers and two tiny, dark, decrepit, and often deserted classrooms. More frequently, though, the college ignores the needs of the majority of its students, preferring not to let the outside world see its deficiencies too clearly.

That is where the dummies come in. Providing one or two classes each semester identified as "remedial" is enough to demonstrate that the college is doing all it can for its "weaker" students and enough to keep the money flowing in. If it admitted, by doing away with dummy classes in English and mathematics, that almost all its students are passengers in the same boat, it might be constrained to spend all that money for a real center, a center that could truly serve the needs of all the students.

In order to give the dummy program the appearance of a true remedial program, the college had attempted to make the zero courses different from the regular freshman courses —not better, just different. In its report to HEW the college announced that it had taken "new approaches to Remedial English and Remedial Mathematics." The college declared that "each course utilized different reference material and a different textbook from those used in Mathematics 1 and English 1 [the regular freshman courses]. Students enrolled in the courses met for five fifty-five minute periods each week with their regular classroom teacher." One does not have to be an educator, however, to realize that there is more to remedial education than a "different textbook" and additional class time. Ironically, although the college does not mention this fact in its report, the extra class time required of the dummies left them no time to attend the reading and speech classes which they needed much more than an extra two hours a week with an English teacher. Thus, the center classes were attended, not by the remedial dummies, for whom they were supposedly designed, but by the regular freshmen.

There was still another financial hitch to Zero English. As long as the dummy classes existed, the college could make a good case for federal funds to pay the salaries of visiting scholars, specialists in remedial education. In a report on a recent school year requesting continued federal support of its visiting scholars, the college declared that "the two visiting scholars are devoting their time to Freshman English and cooperating with remedial programs in Reading and Speech. These programs are structured to assist students in over-coming deficiencies and award no credit. The college is not financially able to continue this program alone." When I read this report at the Division of College Support in Washington, after leaving Thomas College, I recognized immediately that the visiting scholars working on the zero classes of freshman English could not possibly have cooperated to any significant extent with the reading and speech programs, since their students had no time to take reading and speech. Even the regular freshman English classes and the reading and speech classes cooperated only in very informal and sporadic fashion, for the organization of the reading and speech classes as a separate "center," totally independent of the English department, prohibited thorough correlation of the programs. There simply was no one, aside from the president, with the authority to ensure cooperation among the various teachers, and he was too busy.

But who in the world were these visiting scholars? Although I had taught freshman English all year, I had never met them. Matching up the figures listed for the grant with what I knew of Thomas salaries, I realized with a jolt that one of the visiting scholars so devoted to developing the remedial programs might have been me. The college had never reported the identity of its visiting scholars to the Office of Education, but at my request the officer responsible for the Thomas file obtained a list of their names from the school, a list that confirmed my suspicions. I had indeed been an official visiting scholar at Thomas, although no one had bothered to tell me. Even more startling to me was the name of the other visiting scholar who supposedly had worked with me in developing the freshman English and remedial programs. The name listed was Dr. Herman Shurders, but no one by that name was on the faculty during my stay at Thomas. There was, however, a Dr. Herman Schwitters, and since he had been employed at Thomas only two or three years, the administrators might not yet have learned to spell his name correctly. Dr. Schwitters understandably did nothing for the betterment of the English program; he was a professor of chemistry. And at the very time the college was begging for continued federal support of our fine work, I had already quit, with the encouragement of the administration, and Dr. Schwitters had been unceremoniously fired. "These programs as they are functioning and expanding today," the college pleaded in a more recent report, "cannot be continued if Title III support is withdrawn. The college is not financially prepared to fund these programs alone. The remedial programs in Reading and Speech which are most essential will have to be discontinued if present funding is withdrawn."

The programs, like so many at Thomas, existed mainly on paper; but to give the proper impression to any inspector who might happen by, there had to be remedial classes listed in the catalogue, and there had to be students officially classified as dummies. Greeson, of course, couldn't explain that to me, or to anyone. He had to let me go through the motions of my proposal, confident that my plan would be destroyed at some lower level in the pecking order on specious "pedagogical" grounds. When the proposal got through, he was compelled to kill it himself, for his own protection and that of Mr. Baggett. Yet in its official report on my work, the college asserted that I had spent one-fifth of my time during the year on "curriculum development," as the federal Division of College Support expects a visiting scholar to do. Nowhere did it mention that my major proposal for curriculum development had been squashed by the president himself at the behest of a business officer.

No one is ever made the fool without his cooperation. That I had thought myself to be acting in good faith on behalf of sound principles didn't count for much. Baggett and Greeson had banked on my gullibility and my naive, arrogant belief that the college should and would defer to my judgment in this matter. It was a good bet, and when the hand was all over, the house was still flourishing. I had been put in my place and, becoming increasingly distrustful of my own motives, had little fighting spirit left. Worst of all was the knowledge that once again those who suffered most were the students. The dummies had been kept in their place, and I had helped keep them there. Next year there would be a new batch of dummies, and perhaps a new dummy professor. And so all of us—the greedy, the ambitious, the naive—continued to serve the masters.

5

The House Niggers

In his amiable moods, President Greeson was a story-teller; and his favorite story concerned his success as a teacher. During World War II, one of Greeson's fellow soldiers was a man was could neither read nor write. Letters from the man's wife had to be read aloud to him by his buddies. One day, for a joke, they read out to him, instead of the warm words his wife had written, their own version of a "Dear John" letter. For days they enjoyed their joke as the illiterate soldier sunk into deep depression. When he threatened suicide, Greeson decided that the joke had gone far enough; he told the soldier the truth. The illiterate, swept by rage and frustration, decided that he must learn to read and write himself; within three months he had learned—from Simon Greeson. The moral of the story, as Greeson told it, was that one could teach anything to anybody who was highly motivated; the teacher's job was to motivate his students to learn. We listened patiently to that instructive tale many times, but it left one question unanswered. What was to motivate the faculty?

As an administrator, Greeson preached the themes of working together and achieving our goals. But as master of the college, he practiced the role of paternalistic dictator. He treated all the professors as though they were children, sometimes haranguing them, sometimes patting them on the head, but never allowing them freedom of choice or the power of decision. Children, after all, are to be seen, not heard. He preferred to appear as the kindly father, prodding and cajoling the faculty to do his bidding, to do "what is best for the college." Yet he was not one to spare the rod; he was capable of meting out all sorts of punishments—denunciations, threats, demotions, firings—to his naughty children.

One of his most efficient tools in demoralizing the faculty was the faculty meeting. Unlike most colleges that apply the term *faculty* to the instructional staff, Thomas College considered all employees to be members of the faculty. A professor seated at a faculty meeting between a file clerk and a janitor, all of them equally empowered to vote on the curriculum, is not likely to get any high and mighty ideas about himself. No one is interested in the professor's ideas anyway; he has been called to the meeting to listen to the president practice his rhetoric. Like the plantation master who summoned the house slaves to kneel painfully in the corner while he read from the scriptures for their moral edification, Greeson lined up his employees on rows of tortuous folding chairs and talked and talked and talked. At the end of a meeting, physically exhausted and emotionally whipped, the professors crawled out, dragging their professional status behind them. Anyone who had been uppity enough to ask a question of the president would later be called to Greeson's office to be given a "proper understanding" of the issue and of his own status. Anyone who skipped the meeting would be asked to explain his absence, for attendance was required; the president's secretary, like a stern schoolmarm, took the roll in her record book.

When a major foundation gave Thomas a grant to revise the college's administrative and business offices and draw up a manual on the duties and rights of faculty, Greeson himself took charge of the project. Whether the administrative and business operations were revised or not, I don't know; but the faculty did get a guide—only a year after the college reported to HEW that a faculty guide had been distributed. Since it was compiled by Greeson, however, it covered the duties of the president's secretary more thoroughly than it did the rights of faculty; but the duties listed for the faculty revealed that Greeson had even less respect for their skills than for his secretary's. The teachers were instructed to report for school on time, attend their classes regularly, serve on committees when asked, attend all faculty meetings and public functions, and accept no outside employment without the president's consent. There was not a word about the quality of teaching or the development of curricula. And the major duty of teachers was listed as "cooperating fully with the President in promulgating the objectives, purposes and philosophy of the college and defending and furthering the cherished ideals enunciated in the official goals and philosophy of the institution." Proud of his document, the president called a faculty meeting to discuss it; but when teachers pointed out its significant errors and omissions, Greeson angrily closed the meeting. Teachers should be thankful to have a faculty guide at all, he told us. After all, he didn't *have* to give us one. He had taken all the trouble of writing it up for people who didn't even display a proper appreciation of his magnanimity. "You ought to be grateful," he said, "and not try to pick away and find fault with it. You can't be good teachers unless you have a good, positive attitude."

The teachers' impotence was enforced at the departmental level as well. Department chairmen, particularly the older ones, emulated Greeson and took it upon themselves to exercise arbitrary control of their departments. In the English department, the largest of the school, teachers could not request meetings; they could not even add to the meeting agenda, which was composed only of subjects on which the chairman wished to lecture her faculty. About the curriculum, teachers had even less to say; it had been devised years before by the chairman or one of her predecessors. The textbooks, too, had been selected years before by the chairman, and there could be no talk of changing them. It made no difference that many of them were hopelessly out of date. Teachers and students were supposed to study avidly the traditional methods of diagraming sentences because the chairman had never heard of descriptive linguistics or transformational grammar. Students who were hearing rumblings of Black Power, or who were being drafted to serve in a war they did not understand, were expected to read with interest innocuous little stories by Louisa May Alcott and Booth Tarkington. It didn't matter to the chairman that the textbooks had been written for people in another time and of another color. In the freshman English grammar text, an exercise designed to teach the use of logical connectives read: "She had not put up her hair; ————, her hair was straight." According to the answer book, students were supposed to supply a "logical" connective: "therefore," "consequently," or "naturally." Of course, few women "put up" their hair these days; many white women "set" theirs, and many black women "press" theirs—or at least they used to. When black women do not press their hair, it usually appears not naturally straight but naturally "natural." But for years the chairman and her faculty had been drilling black students on that exercise and wondering why it was so hard for them to grasp the logic of things.

Like petty dictators struggling to maintain control, some department chairmen resorted to devious means. Mrs. Hood, chairman of speech, and Dr. Harder, chairman not only of

English but also of the School of Arts and Letters, had created intricate networks of spies and counterspies to make
certain that their directives were enforced. They rigorously
pumped the students for information about their classes:
what texts were being used, what chapters were being covered, what exercises were being assigned. They also employed
informers to foment rebellion against teachers they did not
like, suggesting to the students that certain instructors were
not teaching the "truth." In the case of white instructors
who departed from obsolete methods, they hinted that they
taught "lies" because they "didn't like the colored."

When Dr. Dexter, the young white speech professor,
was assigned to teach a course entitled "Proper Usage of the
English Language," she tried to convey to her students the
important functions of language and the ways in which it
changes with the situation. Adopting the point of view of
descriptive linguistics, she directed the class in research
projects to discover how their own dialects systematically
diverged from certain forms of standard English. The students were interested. Here was something new: their own
speech was not merely "bad English," as they had so often
been told, but a dialect worth studying, a means of learning
something about their own language background and about
the so-called correct English.

The course, however, was not intended to study spoken
language; for years it had been another semester of diagraming the syntax of "correct" English and drilling on elocution;
and Mrs. Hood insisted it remain that way. Dr. Harder, who
was unaware that language patterns are not God-given ab-
solutes and who tried in her own speech to approximate
the syntax of Miltonic verse, sided for once, with her rival,
Mrs. Hood. They didn't understand what Dr. Dexter was
doing, but they knew they didn't like it. They hinted to the
students that Dr. Dexter was a racist who refused to teach
correct speech because she wanted to "keep the colored

down." With Dr. Harder's backing, the students refused to complete the projects Dr. Dexter assigned them. Many of them believed the fantastic tale concocted by Dr. Harder and Mrs. Hood; others found in it a convenient excuse for avoiding their school work. Unfortunately, the defensive fantasy contained a small particle of truth, but Dr. Dexter's prejudice was quite different from the vicious bigotry attributed to her. Rather, her unconscious and subtle racism manifested itself in an involuted, solicitous "kindness" to blacks; she was unable to demand of her black students the performance she might have insisted upon from whites. Her refusal, or inability, to assert her own view in the face of her students' recalcitrance seemed to confirm Mrs. Hood's interpretation. The conjunction of Dr. Dexter's behavior and the Hood-Harder story, like a small spark in a dry forest, produced waste. By midsemester, Dr. Dexter had an insurrection on her hands, and she was powerless to overcome it. For the students, the semester was a loss; for the teacher it was a disaster.

Like faculty heads everywhere, Dr. Harder could have observed the classes taught by her faculty; she could have discussed pedagogical matters with them. But that would have been too open and straightforward. Dr. Harder's own struggle to advance in a white world had taught her that deviousness and subterfuge were the means to success and power. It was too late for her to unlearn the lesson of her seventy-five years' experience.

To make her spy system work, she had to maintain control over the students; an informer must be given incentive. Keeping control of the students was easy. As chairman of the department, Dr. Harder made herself the adviser of every student majoring or minoring in English. She told the students which subjects to take under which instructors. English majors could not take music courses taught by Mr. Hadden because Dr. Harder did not like "that troublemaker," a proud black man. She told the students how many credits they needed in English, and when her requirements differed from those set forth in the college catalogue, her word was law. She could, and did, force students whom she wanted to keep under her wing to return to college semester after semester, earning more credits in English, long after they had fulfilled all the official requirements for graduation. The English students knew that Dr. Harder could determine whether or not they would graduate and when. And so they told her what she wanted to hear, behaved as she wanted them to behave. Why not? Getting an education was all just a game anyway.

Dr. Harder, of course, did not see her own behavior as tyrannical. She was a very devout Christian who believed above all else in performing good works, in sacrificing the self for others—in this case the English majors, whom she regarded as her own "children." To take care of other people, however, regardless of one's good intentions, is to rob them of the opportunity to care for themselves, to make their own choices, as most of the students were eager to do. The English students' choices were constricted by Dr. Harder's profound dedication to "culture." Tragically, to her, "culture" was purely white. Black Americans, she felt, have been held back largely by their inability to acquire "refinement." Having devoted her whole life to bringing culture to black students for the betterment of her race, Dr. Harder was understandably impatient with the foolishness of unrefined people who disagreed with her. In keeping her students out of Mr. Hadden's classes she "saved" them from studying black music; that Hadden took time from studying the classics to discuss African music and jazz constituted, for her, criminal irresponsibility. From her point of view, the racial heritage was not a badge of honor but a stigma. The same feelings prompted her opposition to Dr. Dexter's speech class and to my plan for abolishing the dummy English course; the students, she contended, must be told that their English is bad and taught to use the language correctly. The same feelings caused her to see young Dr. Norden's black pride as dangerous wrong-mindedness and to oppose her at every turn. And she kept her favorite students at Thomas, not to harass them, but to teach them all she could about English and piety and humility, the lessons she had learned so long ago. She was not a demon; she was a kindhearted, motherly old woman who continued to sacrifice for her people, not knowing that the times had passed her by.

While Dr. Harder and Mrs. Hood improvised their own means of humbling the faculty, some methods—like the faculty meeting—were general. One of the most subtle but most effective was the requisition form. To obtain any material—a pencil, a paper clip, a sheet of carbon paper—a teacher had to fill out a requisition form in quadruplicate. Each requisition had to be approved by the departmental chairman, the dean of studies, the president, and the vice-president. The process of approving a requisition and filling the order might consume weeks, even months. Early in the year, I requisitioned several reams of ditto paper and a large box of ditto master sheets, more or less standard equipment for a teacher of English composition. Two months later I received the ditto masters, but my request for ditto paper had been turned down because I had failed to specify the color I wanted. Since the ditto masters obviously were useless without the paper to print them on, I filled out another requisition, carefully specifying white paper 8½ by 11 inches. Weeks elapsed before I received notice that my request had been approved and would be filled as soon as the college bought some ditto paper. The paper eventually was delivered, but not until I had relinquished my plans for using it; the semester was over. In the classroom, I had improvised, knowing all along that the methods I was forced to use were not so effective as those I might have used if I had received the materials and supplies I wanted. That knowledge was demoralizing enough. But it was even more demoralizing to know that a secretary could simply unlock the supply cabinet and take the supplies that I, as a professor, had to requisition in quadruplicate. In the end, the fight for the ditto materials proved to be meaningless anyway: the ditto machine that I was allowed to use was broken. My subsequent requisition for repair of the ditto machine was approved and supposedly filled, but when the machine was returned from the shop, it was still broken in the same place. The college did own a ditto machine that worked perfectly, but I was forbidden to use that one. It was reserved for the administrators and their secretaries and was used to print important materials, such as the requisition forms.

Another kind of requisition had to be submitted in quadruplicate to get money for traveling to professional conferences. Each department had funds for this purpose in its budget, and in addition the college had received several generous grants from educational foundations to be allocated to faculty members attending professional meetings. The travel money, however, became another of the administration's tools of tyranny. They held it before the faculty like candy before children; the good children were rewarded, the bad ones did without. Dr. Norden, who quickly had been categorized as a bad child, submitted one form after another, and each was rejected on some specious grounds. Her application to go to Chicago for an educators' conference on "Humanizing Education" was refused by Dr. Harder because the conference topic had "nothing to do with teaching English." Besides, Dean Butler informed her, the college did not have the money to send someone all the way to Chicago. Both Dr. Norden and I requested money to go to the national convention of the College Language Association, a prominent organization of language teachers from black colleges. The conference promised to be exciting and valuable, centering on linguistic problems of black dialects and the application of linguistics to the teaching of standard English to nonstandard speakers. Yet Dr. Harder vetoed our request on the grounds that the conference was to be "on linguistics instead of English." Since the administration liked to give a semblance of fairness to its allotment of the travel money, however, one of Dr. Norden's requisitions was finally approved. It was the one she had submitted as a joke. She was given thirty dollars to attend a conference at a neighboring state university on "Place Names in Our State." But no one mistook the semblance of fairness for the real thing. In the spring, the four-man physical education department jetted all the way to San Francisco for a week-long conference on physical fitness. According to their report, they had a "real good time."

Although the administrators were expert at reducing professors to limp and impotent frustration, their techniques were often superfluous, for many professors were already convinced of their own inferiority. A large number of the faculty were Thomas College graduates, ill qualified to find teaching jobs at other schools. Several faculty members who were well prepared academically were recent immigrants from foreign countries, some of them totally unintelligible to their students; although they might have obtained research positions, few schools would have hired them for the classroom. The position of such teachers at the college was so tenuous that they willingly and gratefully stayed in the lowly place to which they were relegated. It was the uppity teachers whom the college worried about, those few well-qualified and unattached people who could move to better positions elsewhere and, after a year, did so. During their brief stay, they suffered most of the administration's repressive attempts at brainwashing. The barrage served two purposes: it kept the uppity ones in their place for the time being, and it encouraged them to leave at the end of the year.

When teachers remain in a college for a number of years, they may gain a vested interest in the success of the institution and its students. They become familiar with the full resources of the college and the community and can use them to advantage in their teaching. They come to know the students intimately and can more accurately anticipate their needs and assess their progress. They have time to experiment in the classroom, testing out methods that work and those that don't, discovering how to improve their classes and the curriculum. They get to know their colleagues and learn how to collaborate with them. Aware of these benefits of having a stable faculty, most colleges try to retain good teachers for many years. Many colleges, believing that a teacher needs at least two or three years to ease into the life of the institution, try to retain most of their faculty members for three years before passing judgment upon them. But not Thomas. It hustled its faculty in and out like so many slaves on the auction block.

To the Thomas administrators, a long-term teacher, thoroughly familiar with the institution, constituted a threat. For one thing, having learned his way around, he might not be so easy to manipulate. Having some seniority, he might want to have his say. He might even conceive some ideas about how the college should be run. In any case, it would require some effort to keep him in his place. The young teachers were the worst. Every one of them had big ideas for changing the school; all objected to one time-honored procedure or another. If they stayed at the college and organized, the administration might be in real trouble. It might well have a full-scale revolution on its hands. It was easier—and in the long run safer—to get rid of them. So Thomas harassed its teachers until they resigned or—if all else failed—it fired them.

When I joined the Thomas faculty, it consisted of forty-two professors. Only twenty-seven of them had been on the faculty the previous year; only fifteen had been at Thomas two years or more. And by the end of that school year, at least half the teachers who had been at Thomas two years or more had resigned or been fired. Between 1962 and 1970 the faculty had grown from thirty-four to forty-two, but only five teachers had remained throughout the eight-year period.

If Thomas were replacing poor teachers with better ones, its astonishing faculty turnover rate might be understandable. But that clearly was not the case. Thomas did dismiss a few teachers generally believed to be incompetent, but its chief targets were some of its best teachers. Over the years, the English department had fired a series of excellent one-year teachers, retaining from year to year four professors whose training and ability could generously be called marginal. The science chairman, an outstanding teacher and retired chairman of the chemistry department at a well-known public university, was summarily fired after two years. Professors holding excellent credentials from very good schools were fired wholesale. Meanwhile, professors with bachelor's or master's degrees from questionable colleges—such as Thomas itself—were retained. Of the five long-term professors on campus, two were approaching senility and a third—an antique gentleman who habitually slept through the classes he was supposed to be teaching—obviously had entered it. Clearly the five had been retained not for their ability but for their docility.

That docility qualified them for the most powerful positions on the faculty; they were appointed by the president to head departments or one of the five schools of the college, exercising complete and more or less arbitrary control of teachers and courses under their command. One of them was Dr. Harder, chairman of the English department and also of the School of Arts and Letters, positions that put her in control not only of the English department but also of the departments of French, Spanish, speech, art, and music. Another old retainer was chairman of the School of Social Studies, which included the history department, chaired by Mrs. Butler. A third, the old coach, chaired the physical education department and the School of Education. Both the department of secretarial science and the School of Business were headed by Mrs. Greeson. That these department and school heads remained in office indefinitely "at the discretion of the president" ensured that their power could be exercised only downward, upon their lowly faculties. The arrangement must have been very gratifying to the president. Having his rubber stamps in important offices left only one section of the college imperfectly controlled, the School of Science, headed temporarily by a visiting scholar who was planning some revisions. But Greeson got around that challenge; at the end of the year he fired not only the school head but also every one of the school's faculty.

Despite its revolving-door policy for faculty members, Thomas continued to collect federal money to improve its faculty. For several years, HEW has provided funds for visiting scholars at Thomas. As I have noted, however, Thomas did not tell the teachers hired with this money that they were official visiting scholars. Since they could hardly have fulfilled HEW expectations, of which they had not been informed, it seems unlikely that the visiting scholars did much to improve Thomas. I know I certainly didn't.

HEW has also given the college money to hire national teaching fellows. National teaching fellowships, according to a government publication, are "to be awarded to highly qualified graduate students and junior faculty members of established colleges and universities" so that they may teach at institutions like Thomas. The Division of College Support assumes that the presence of national teaching fellows on campus will free less qualified teachers for a year or two of graduate study; when the fellow has completed his service —of no more than two years—the regular faculty member whom he has temporarily replaced will be better qualified to carry on. Alternatively, the recipient college might hire fellows to teach basic courses in fields in which it does not offer a major and cannot attract experienced professors; at Thomas a graduate student might have taught introductory courses in physics, art, or any of a dozen other disciplines. In any case, it is assumed that the addition of new faculty from established schools in other parts of the country will revitalize the institution. Thomas, however, has deployed its teaching fellowships in strange ways.

During the first year in which Thomas participated in the program, the Division of College Support provided $30,000 to hire four outside fellows. Instead, the college split the money six ways—or five ways, according to another report covering the same period—paying the full salaries of two women who were *already* on the faculty, a speech teacher and a home economics teacher, and the partial salaries of new teachers in music, math, chemistry, and art, one of them a Thomas graduate. Receiving $15,000 for two new fellows the second year, Thomas again used the money to pay the speech teacher and the home economics teacher. In the third year, it used a grant of $14,200 to continue paying the same home economics teacher and to pay a biology teacher. For the fourth year, with $13,800 in its pocket, it fired the biology teacher and hired someone else; but it continued paying the same home economics teacher.

Through the national teaching fellowships, the college did attract some new faculty members, but clearly it did not use the fellowships as they were intended to be used. One recipient was a Thomas graduate and another—the home economics teacher who has been on the rolls for at least four years—is a local resident, daughter-in-law of the head of the college store and daughter of the head of the college laundry.

The college's reports to the Division of College Support indicate that it paid the speech teacher, an assistant professor, $7,500 at a time when the average salary for that rank supposedly was $6,600. That she should have received more than the average is conceivable, for she was white, and the college regularly pays higher salaries to whites than to blacks. But the home economics teacher, an instructor and black, supposedly was paid the same salary, although the average pay for one with her rank was $5,400. Over the years her reported salary has gone down—to $7,100 and then $6,900—but it is still far above the college's range for instructors, $5,000–$5,900, figures that are themselves probably higher than the actual salaries paid. The home economics teacher, a local black woman, certainly would not expect to earn as much as $7,000 a year in her Southern home town. Why has she been kept on a fellowship all these years?

Despite its idiosyncratic use of the funds for visiting scholars and national teaching fellows, the college continues to write enthusiastic reports to the Division of College Support about the division's aid to the college. In a recent report, Dean Butler wrote:

> Evaluation of the strengths of the continually developing and expanding institution evidence improvement at Thomas College mainly as a result of: a dynamic program for instructional staff development; . . . the excellently qualified staff which claim nearly 50 per cent possessing the doctorate degree; the services of visiting scholars and national teaching fellows.

The federal agency asks the college for no information about the qualifications and performance of the visiting scholars and national teaching fellows; nor does it ask the scholars and fellows themselves for reports, as might be expected when it is paying their salaries. It simply assumes that the college will use the money appropriately and advantageously, although its own experience in prosecuting college officials who proved to be white-collar criminals might indicate that not all colleges will do so. Indeed, the Division of College Support seems at times to enjoy its blissful ignorance; it does not even ask the college for figures on its rate of faculty turnover, figures that would reflect significantly on the quality of institutional life. Free of bothersome statistics, the federal officer can be gratified by Dean Butler's report that "Attention is . . . focused on faculty development." In fact, the only aspect of the faculty that the college wanted to develop was obedience.

Reduced to submission by circumstances or direct attack, the powerless professors took out their frustrations on one another. Faculty-room gossip—a conversational genre seldom distinguished for its human kindness—descended to viciousness and obscenity. Hours were spent over cooling coffee cups in freewheeling speculation about the sexual attributes and exercises of colleagues. Powdery skeletons were raked from nearly forgotten closets and reassembled bone by bone. In their spare time, teachers pumped students for information about other faculty members, embellished the news, and polished their monologues for the next kaffeeklatsch. Hostile and defensive as they were, their attacks had no limits. The serious illness of a colleague prompted ribald tales and laughter about the erotic indulgence that had sapped his health. Vulgarity passed for humor and lewdness for wit, and since several faculty members spent more time in the coffee room than they did in the classroom, they became highly skilled at character assassination. The least secure among the faculty joined the coffee crowd, presumably on the theory that if they were among the talkers they could not be talked about. And so the game went on.

But the teachers saved most of their hostility for the only group that appeared to have less power than they: the students. Almost everyone talked endlessly about the extraordinary stupidity of the students, both behind their backs and in their presence. The public attitude of almost every professor maintained that the students were hopeless ninnies who would soon come to a bad end anyway but who, through rigorous discipline by the faculty, might at least be taught to wipe their noses.

Most of the black teachers, particularly the older ones, had undergone a long struggle to get where they were. It is not easy to climb into the black bourgeoisie. But they had believed in the American dream and the white man's slogan that integration would come naturally when blacks had been educated sufficiently to deserve a place at the table. They had graduated from college and many of them from graduate school. They dressed well and conservatively. They kept up their property. They had even learned to speak like the white man and were never loud in public places. All that the white man had admonished them to do, they did. Still, whitey treated them just as he had before, blocking their entrance at this door and that, confining them to their own ghetto. That they were still treated like niggers was explained by the white man's inability to distinguish between one grade of black and another; it was the lower-class blacks —the "dumb, lazy niggers"—who were holding back the whole race. The middle-class teachers sometimes spoke angrily against whitey, but in their innermost hearts they blamed their continued oppression, not on white racism, but upon the lower-class members of their own race.

Consequently, they were much more impatient with their students than were the white instructors. They selected a few dutiful and tractable students as favorites, for such students were simply junior versions of the teachers, subscribing to the same values and myths; but the mass of students they insulted, abused, and denounced as "dumb niggers." Their resentment was increased by the fact that the students were receiving state or federal aid to attend school. In their day, no one had helped blacks along. Now any "fool" who wanted to attend college could get "a free ride." They had pulled themselves up by their "own bootstraps"; now all these dumb kids were being "coddled." The psychological dynamics of self-hate and of the enmity between the black teachers and their students are complex indeed. Generations of white oppression have produced some grotesque attitudes, such as that of a black professor who complained angrily to me, "Most of these niggers are so stupid they ought to be taken out and shot."

Despising the students as they did, many faculty members could not be bothered to teach them anything. Year after year, they sauntered to class with the same dog-eared lecture notes; in some cases, one suspects that the notes were those they had taken down in their own student days, perhaps thirty or forty years before. One of the student counselors planned to offer a course in sociology, although he had never taught before; his slight acquaintance with sociology had been gained many years before in an undergraduate survey course, but he was confident that he could teach the course well because he "still had the notes."

The conception of the process of education as the transferring of notes from one tablet to another is, of course, appalling to anyone who has more than a nodding acquaintance with learning. But it is quite understandable when one considers the educational experience of many of those who are now faculty members. Many of the older blacks who have completed advanced college degrees did so by rote memorization of a culture far removed from their own experience. Dr. Harder, for example, grew up in the rural South but, driven by the ambitions of her schoolteacher mother, she toiled through a small Northern university. Suddenly exposed to accents and words she had never encountered before, she was lost. Her immediate task was to learn what all those words meant. Yet she smiled sweetly through every racial slur—even when the college denied her permission to use the "white" locker room during physical education class— and spent her evenings studying the dictionary, so dedicated was she to acquiring "culture." Who could have the heart to tell her that she would never make it? So they passed her on, giving her a bachelor's degree and then a master's degree, knowing that she could do their reputation no harm since, no matter what degrees she held, she would not be allowed to teach in a white school.

Then her money ran out, and she went to work as a teacher, saving what she could from her small salary against the day when she could go back to school. At last, after fifteen years, she entered another small Northern university to study for her doctorate. When he discovered she was a Negro, her adviser warned her to drop out. No Negro, he told her, had ever gained a Ph.D. at the college; it couldn't be done. But she must have shown him that gracious smile and rolled out a sample of her astonishing vocabulary. So they let her sit in the back of the room, carefully segregated from the rest of the class, all those years, while she dutifully memorized the required material and set it out in her cautious hand on examination papers. No one told her. Everyone passed her on. And finally, when she had paid her dues, they sent her back to her people in the South, a certified distinguished scholar. Once, when I substituted for her in her Milton class, she lent me her textbook. In the margins of *Paradise Lost* she had written out in a precise hand the definitions of all the words she could not remember.

For more than twenty years those definitions have been transferred from her margins to the notebooks of her students, and none of them has understood Milton's lost paradise—or their own, which the white man has hurled them from. Dr. Harder genuinely tries, according to her lights, to teach the students something; she wants to make them as successful as she is herself. But like her colleagues who simply cannot be bothered, she comes to class with her yellowed notes and reads from them. She even addresses her faculty at department meetings from a carefully prepared script. That is the only method with which she and her colleagues can feel secure, for it is all they have. It is the only kind of education America has let them have.

Those who have studied the psychology of slaves report that the slave, powerless to help himself and dependent for subsistence upon his master, comes to identify his own interests with those of the master. As the master fares, so will the slave. Similarly, the slavish faculty at Thomas identified themselves with the administration, and despite all their vocal complaints, finally took the side of the administration against the students. Having no real power, however, they—again like slaves—tended to ape the superficial characteristics of the master.

Some, like Mrs. Hood, played the grande dame, forcing students to wait upon them like personal body servants. She could not forgive her husband, the former president, for dying and leaving her a lowly professor instead of a powerful president's wife. Fiercely, she tried to prolong her reign. She drove up each day in her astonishing white Cadillac, pushed the button to roll down the automatic window, and shrieked in her best stage accent at the nearest male student, "Boy! Come open this door. Have you no mannahs?" Although she was a tiny, frail woman, her theatrical training had given her a commanding presence. Wherever she went on the campus, she led a grand procession. She marched—as best she could on her stiletto heels—with her nose in the air and her coat flung about her shoulders like a scarlet cape, preceded and followed by a scurrying entourage of "boys," some of whom were thirty-year-old Vietnam veterans, carrying her books and her purse, opening and closing doors, and on rainy days holding an umbrella over her shining wig.

When she departed in her white coach, flinging the red dust in their faces, her footmen snickered and giggled; but the next day they would be her footmen, nonetheless.

Although she mistook form for substance, Mrs. Hood was not a stupid woman. Like Dr. Harder, she was the product of her Southern miseducation. Deprived of any knowledge of her black cultural heritage, she had acquired the values of the white society, the values held up as those of a superior culture. But what the white society offered with one hand, it took away with the other, segregating the black society and systematically depriving blacks of any real achievement in terms of white values. The trappings of culture existed within the "great books"—which Mrs. Hood read avidly—and not in her own experience. And so Mrs. Hood dutifully taught her speech classes about the superb oratory of Demosthenes, Daniel Webster, and Winston Churchill, but never mentioned Frederick Douglass or Martin Luther King, Jr. or Malcolm X. Her modern drama students read Thornton Wilder but not Lorraine Hansberry. So completely had she been "whitewashed" that she vehemently opposed the teaching of black literature at the college, asserting that only "great" literature should be taught. When Dr. Dexter, the white speech teacher, gave her a copy of a play by Imamu Amiri Baraka (LeRoi Jones), she haughtily returned it after reading a few pages; it was full of "filthy" language. So she continued to put her students through three months of arduous daily rehearsals for the school plays, teaching them her version of British elocution—even if the play were set in Keokuk, Iowa. And the students continued to appear in meaningless, sentimental comedies about the white middle class. After each performance, she appeared center stage to receive a massive bouquet of roses amid general applause and everyone pretended that the latest production had been another triumph of the theater and a credit to the college. In a society that offered equal opportunity, Mrs. Hood might have been an actress; instead she was a professor. And perhaps more effectively than any other professor at the college, she taught her students the lesson of their lives—to be humble sycophants.

Mrs. Hood was an extreme case. Many other black professors had been less perfectly whitewashed. Although they had lived most of their lives in terms of white middle-class values, they had not achieved success in the white world. They were college professors—but only at an obscure black college. And while they were respected by older members of the black community, they did not automatically receive the adulation of young blacks. Now entering middle age, they began to suspect that they had sacrificed their lives to false gods. In trying to be white they had missed something that was rightfully theirs, something distinctively black. This uncertainty about their own identity was expressed in a curious hostility toward the students. On the one hand, they preached even more strenuously the values they themselves had found hollow. If young people could be schooled to live according to those values, the values would be, in a sense, vindicated. That young people might choose to live differently was a challenge to their whole existence, a statement that their own lives had been meaningless.

On the other hand, such professors recognized that many young people *were* choosing to live differently. They met that threat with open hostility. A business professor liked to display a fat roll of bills to his class, telling the young men that such wealth would never be theirs because they were too stupid to learn business. The young track coach forced his athletes to shave their heads for "hygienic" reasons; no young man with a beard, a mustache, or an Afro hair style could be on the team. Often the hostility—particularly between the male professors and the young men—was more overtly sexual. A handsome student who was openly proud of his manhood and his blackness could not easily pass business. Usually the professor's control over the student's course grade was enough to ensure conformity and subservience, but where professorial power alone was inadequate, young black pride could be suppressed by physical violation, by cropping the young man's head.

The female professors who felt similarly threatened took a different approach. They, too, preached the whitewashed values, but from those girls who remained unconvinced they desperately tried to win approval. The very few proud young black women on the campus were a different breed altogether from the rural Southern girls, with their pressed hair and compressed minds, and it was no coincidence that the proud young women were also the most intelligent. Mrs. Hood coerced them to perform in all her plays, while Dr. Harder and Mrs. Washington fought to get them into their classes.

One of these girls enrolled in my literature class, where she quickly distinguished herself as one of the brightest students I had ever had during many years of teaching at several schools. I asked her to stop by my office sometime, but it took her two months to get there. We talked about her interest in doing graduate work, and I gave her a book on graduate opportunities for minority-group students, offering to recommend her. During our conversation she explained that before she had been able to come to my office to talk with me she had had to make sure that I would not "put her through changes." She had had to know that my purpose was not to force her into a play or a testimonial to my teaching and my classes. She had experienced a great deal of trouble, she confided, because she was incapable of giving solicited tributes. That explained why, although I had found her to be open and forthright, I had so often been warned by my older colleagues that she had a "bad attitude" and should not be given an A grade until she changed her manner. So far she had not catered to her professors;

she had simply done her school work brilliantly. That conference was our first and last; she went her way and I mine, and she continued to do superb work in my class. Occasionally, I suggested to her after class the titles of books I thought would interest her; she always wrote them down and thanked me, but she never told me if she read them and I had no need to ask. At the end of the semester, I gave her an A grade that may well have been the first A she had received during her three years as a Thomas student.

There were some professors at the college who did not have to put the students down. But to many of them, their work at the college was just a job; their real interests were elsewhere. They came to school and taught their classes well, but since they immediately left the campus again, their influence on the students was negligible. Others, however, professed to be interested only in bettering the lot of the students and spent all their time working on the students' behalf.

The most energetic of this group was Mr. Rogers, the young white man who chaired the education department. He was an excellent teacher, admired by his students both for the quality of his classes and for his fairness. He expected his students to work, but he played no games with them. Outside the classroom, he was always engaged in some project for improving the quality of the students' education and their lives at the school. He had devoted months to revising the education department's requirements and curriculum. He worked closely with his faculty to make sure the courses were well taught and the students treated fairly. He supervised many student groups and served on every committee designed to improve the college, often as chairman, usually as the only committee member who actually did any work. His dedication was extraordinary; indeed, the college was his whole life. In the grand liberal tradition, he fancied himself a gifted white man sacrificing his future to help his less fortunate colored brethren. He was, in his own eyes, the Albert Schweitzer of Thomas College.

Greeson, unfortunately, saw that quality in Rogers and used it. Greeson suggested to Rogers what needed to be done, Rogers did it, and Greeson slapped him on the back. Yet Rogers knew that Greeson needed him. Intelligent, articulate, efficient, eminently responsible, and white, Rogers was just the sort of person Greeson needed to show off to visiting consultants and prospective benefactors. Greeson's need of him gave Rogers a bit of leverage, which he used discreetly to reform his department and to initiate courses in the history of black education. Ironically, young black professors, just as able as Rogers and every bit as committed to the students and to reform, accomplished much less and stayed only briefly; for while the dynamic "show white" was an asset to Greeson, an equally dynamic black was a menace.

There was no question that Rogers's projects had improved the quality of the students' education, at least in the education department, and that he had protected many students from administrative harassment. Yet the students left his education class to diagram sentences with Dr. Harder or carry Mrs. Hood's satchel or shave their heads for the next track meet, while he trotted off to get some more suggestions from President Greeson. The actual changes he had made on the plantation were miniscule; it was as though he had transferred a few of the slaves from harvesting cotton to the relatively easier task of harvesting tobacco—but only because the master wanted to start growing some tobacco anyway.

There were black teachers, too, who apparently behaved selflessly, dedicating their lives to the students. One whom the students particularly worshiped was Mr. Hadden of the music department. Looking much younger than his forty-some years, he was handsome, apparently hip, and sported the only professorial Afro—though a modest one—on campus. More important, he was gifted with infinite sensitivity to the students—so much so that almost everyone recorded A's in his classes. If the students earned all those good grades, though, it was because Mr. Hadden's courses were not just interesting; they were fun. There were jazz records along with Beethoven in music appreciation, and in a special course on black arts there was more jazz, as well as plays and paintings done by black artists. Mr. Hadden's classes were virtually the only ones in which black kids could learn of black achievement. There, with much to feed upon, pride could grow.

Pride could grow, too, in Mr. Hadden's choir, which he rehearsed incessantly and which consequently sang very well. Only Mr. Hadden could have induced students to labor so long over obscure classical music and songs from light opera. Occasionally he programed a spiritual, but mostly the chorus was compelled to sing what Dr. Harder and President Greeson called "good music."

Mr. Hadden, however, was not trained as a choir director. He had studied to be a concert pianist, but he had no piano students at Thomas. Although he was by far the best pianist in his department, he had to teach all the courses in music appreciation, theory, and history. The three women on the music faculty, who didn't know enough about music to teach those courses, gave the piano lessons.

So Mr. Hadden was dissatisfied with his position. Like Mr. Rogers, he spoke frequently of the excellent offers he had received from other colleges, but like Rogers, he couldn't leave Thomas. He didn't seem to need the adulation of students and faculty as Rogers did, but he did need the safe haven of Thomas. Frequently, he recalled his student days at a Northern university with a distinguished music department. There, he had reveled in his music, but he had been uneasy as the lone black in a white world; and there, where the color line was less clearly demarcated but no less real than in his native South, he hadn't known how to behave. The isolation and the confusion were too much for him. As soon as he finished his degree, he returned to the South as a music teacher. In the South he had drifted through the past twenty years, dreaming wistfully of the opportunities he might have had in the North. Reluctant to admit to his students that he had given up, he told them of the struggles of black musicians to find work in the North. Oh, there were black jazz musicians, but theirs wasn't "real music." And there was an occasional Marian Anderson or Leontyne Price, but their success amounted to nothing but tokenism. Mr. Hadden may have been right about the music world. But unintentionally he convinced his students that, no matter what their talents, they should resign themselves to being public school music teachers. The pride he gave with one hand he unwittingly took away with the other.

Mr. Rogers and Mr. Hadden and a few others were, at least, fine teachers. Most of the professors at Thomas were not. It is difficult to say what constitutes "good teaching." There are probably as many different definitions as there are good teachers. But if good teaching means providing students with an opportunity to grow, the teacher must first believe in the possibility of growth, and he must somehow communicate that belief to his students. Much more is involved than a superficial positive attitude, for as people think, so they behave. The ways in which teachers behave in the classroom are signals to the students, invitations to respond in certain modes. For most students the pattern of invitation and response is set very early in the elementary schools. Preconditioned by his IQ scores and by faculty gossip, the second-grade teacher treats Johnny much as his first-grade teacher did. Johnny quickly learns what behavior his teachers expect of him and responds accordingly.

Most of the Johnnies who grew up to come to Thomas College had long been classified as "dumb." More important, the faculty expected them to be dumb. Some openly called the students dumb niggers, while others gave more subtle cues. Mrs. Washington assigned her classes a few pages of the text each day to be read for the next class meeting, then devoted the next meeting to reading the assigned pages aloud to the class, pausing only to define the difficult words. Her method clearly declared to the students that she considered them incapable of reading the text and looking up unfamiliar words themselves, and the students, knowing that she really didn't expect them to do the assignments, didn't do them. Mrs. Washington then used the fact that they didn't read the assignments as evidence of their stupidity and justification for her method of teaching. Students who have learned during twelve years in the public schools that they are expected to be stupid are quick to pick up cues such as Mrs. Washington offered them.

But there was at least one student who went through the most amazing transformation I have ever seen. Arnold was assigned to my remedial English class and to Mr. Hadden's music appreciation class, where he sat listening but pretending to be half-asleep. Occasionally, he tried to say something, but neither Mr. Hadden nor I could understand a word he uttered; he scarcely opened his mouth, and the words slipped out in a jumbled blur. At last, concluding that he suffered from a speech impediment, Mr. Hadden referred him to the speech laboratory for remedial help, explaining that he needed to be able to understand him because he knew that Arnold had so many important things to say. Almost immediately we both noticed a marked improvement in his speech, and as we began to understand his words we encouraged him to speak more in class. His classmates, too, began to seek him out for their debating and discussion teams in English class. We noticed physical changes as well: he stood up straight, threw his shoulders back, and abandoned his shuffle for a long stride; we realized that he was much taller than he had appeared. By the end of the semester, he had shifted gradually from the back corner of the room to a seat in the front row; there he perched on the edge of his chair, alert, articulate, clearly enjoying the class and himself. At the end of the semester, when we congratulated the speech teacher on her work, we learned that Arnold had never gone to the speech lab.

What had happened to Arnold? The most obvious answer was that he was black, as black a Negro as I have ever seen. And being that color, he had been subjected to the brainwashed Negro's prejudice against the darker members of his own race. From his earliest years in school, Arnold had been dismissed by his Negro teachers who favored their lighter-skinned pupils. Relegated to the back row psychologically as well as physically, he had remained there. No one ever listened to him, so—remarkable as it may seem—he quite literally lost the ability to speak intelligibly. When he at last found some people who wanted to listen to him, he learned how to speak to them. And then we discovered not only that Arnold could speak clearly but also that he was exceptionally sensitive, intelligent, and a born leader. The most important point, however, was not that those of us around him discovered the real Arnold, but that Arnold himself did. In three months, before our astonished eyes, a wiped-out nigger had grown into a proud and beautiful black man.

I have never seen a case so extreme as Arnold's before or since, and I do not mean to suggest that all students are potential Arnolds; but unless a teacher behaves as though every one of his students might be Arnold, he will never unearth the one who is. Unless he believes deeply that every student carries within himself the ability to grow, he will stunt the growth of all of them. And the most heinous fault of almost all the teachers at Thomas was that they did not believe.

Without that belief, teachers can make no commitment to their students or to the art of teaching. The job becomes simply a series of tasks performed for money or status. Being uninvolved, the teacher goes through the motions of the classroom, repeating the same old ineffective techniques and methods from year to year. In one's personal life, such compulsive repetition of ineffective behavior would be regarded as aberrant. In the classroom, however, it is considered normal, or even—by those who exalt order and discipline—exemplary. At Thomas, it was the ideal. Dean Butler's plan to require every teacher to follow an established course outline year after year would have made repetition the rule. The dean, like most of his faculty, considered knowledge to be a finite body of absolute truth and the process of education to be the memorization of those truths. Thus, a course of lectures in physics prepared in 1940 could still be presented in 1980; the lecturer might have to retire, but if he bequeathed his notes to his successor, the lectures could go on and on. And well-prepared lectures filled the entire fifty-minute class period, leaving no time for students' questions, since what students wanted to know was so obviously irrelevant to their education.

The course outlines, the lectures, and the textbooks became shields for the professor to hide behind. They provided his defense against self-exposure, against the need to confront the students as fellow human beings. And most of the teachers, insecure in their positions and uncertain of their subject matter, were terribly afraid of such confrontations. The only authority they possessed at Thomas was authority over the students, and they fought to retain that power by constantly reasserting it, by repeatedly humiliating and humbling the students. This battle for supremacy raged in the classroom, where no challenge to the professor's absolute knowledge and authority could be permitted. Defensive professors usually perceived a student's question as a power play and instead of an answer returned a reprimand or a sarcastic remark about the student's ignorance—particularly if the teacher didn't know the answer himself.

Although the right to question was denied to the students, the teachers retained that prerogative of their superior position. They had learned in their education courses that asking questions of the students is a sound teaching method, producing the illusion of democratic participation in the classroom activity. But in the mouth of an insecure teacher, the question also becomes a defensive weapon. He asks only questions that have "correct" answers and refuses to accept alternative suggestions. In lecturing to her freshman English class on the evils of materialism, Dr. Harder asked rhetorically whether the students would prefer the salvation of their souls to a million dollars. When one young man responded that he would take the million dollars, Dr. Harder assured him that he did not mean what he had said. When he insisted on his preference she summoned him to her office for a private lecture on the error of his ways. The next day he was permitted to stand before the class and apologize for his ignorance, expressing his hope that by getting a good education he would learn "the correct values." Of course, the apologetic young man and his classmates, hiding their snickers behind their hands, took it all as a great joke on Dr. Harder, who apparently believed the apology to be sincere. Yet they had learned that their almighty professors, like their high school teachers, sought not an honest answer but the "correct" one. And they had learned again that right answers in the classroom had nothing whatsoever to do with their own feelings or their own experience.

So the faculty conducted the students through a series of games, the object of which was not the transmission of knowledge but the retention of power. What was needed more than anything else was openness between faculty and students, an openness that would have enabled them to perceive their common interest in escaping the yoke of the master. But too few of the professors understood who they themselves were and what they were about to be honest with their students or with themselves. Where there is no honesty, no openness, no authentic life, there can be only games. And so, like the house niggers and the field niggers of old, faculty and students continued to do battle with one another, never admitting that they were all slaves together, while the master smiled from the cool veranda.

6

The Field Niggers

On the ante-bellum plantation, no one's lot was worse than the field niggers', although it was on their sweating backs that the whole system rested. Similarly, Thomas was built upon the humbled backs of its students.

Any college, by definition, must have a student body, but the students at Thomas were almost an afterthought. Like the field niggers, they were expected to do what they were told and to keep their place. Poorly housed, inadequately fed, economically exploited, they were not allowed to grumble. If they did their work grudgingly or inefficiently, they could be tolerated—as long as they kept smiling and shuffling along. But if they turned surly, they were sent "down the river." The master's benevolence toward these inferior creatures was an act of Christian charity; ingratitude could not be borne. Naturally, ignorant and inferior as they were thought to be, the students had no rights at all.

The college gained its power over the students' lives by reducing them to childlike dependence; almost every one of the 500 students relied more or less completely upon the college for financial support. Almost all of them came from

Southern rural or small-town families that could not have afforded to send their children to college. Indeed, for many such families, losing the child's labor when he left home for college was a financial burden in itself. In 1968, only 4 per cent of the Thomas student body came from families that had an annual income of $7,500 or more, and there is no record of the number of children included in those relatively high-income families. The families of only 6 per cent of the student body enjoyed an annual income between $6,000 and $7,500. Ninety per cent of the students came from families receiving an income of less than $6,000, and 46 per cent from families receiving less than $3,000. By 1971, the figures had grown slightly worse. The college reported to the federal government that "students enrolled at Thomas College are Negroes from low-income families. The families of 49 per cent of the students receive an annual income below $3,000. The families of 42 per cent of the students receive an income under $6,000." What the college meant, of course, is that 42 per cent of the students' families received incomes *between* $3,000 and $6,000; thus, the actual percentage of students' families *below* the $6,000 income level was 91 per cent. And although the college reports no figures on family size, most of the students come from large families.

The families are willing to sacrifice, however, believing that the child's college education will be his passport to a better life. The college offers the children an opportunity most of the parents have never had, and the parents consequently regard the school with awe, deference, and humble gratitude. They exert enormous pressure upon their children, often the first of the family line to attend college, to do as they are told so they can "get educated." The parents' attitude emphatically reinforces a manner the students have already learned, a manner that is fully exploited by the college: the Southern Negro's traditional deference to his elders.

For several years, Thomas has reported that all of its students receive some form of financial aid. Recently, it reported that "an analysis of the financial aid program of the institution demonstrates that 100 per cent of our students receive 90 per cent financial aid." Many Thomas students, however, would be eligible for loans and even scholarships at other, better colleges. A great many colleges and universities now have special programs for promising black students who, because of poor public school training and low family income, cannot meet the usual admission standards and fees. Others have generous scholarship funds specifically for black and other minority-group students. Although many Thomas students probably could have qualified for such programs, they knew nothing about them; their high school guidance counselor—if they had one—had directed them toward the lowly occupations traditionally open to Southern blacks. And in a few cases, the educated parents of the brightest youngsters deliberately kept them out of better colleges, where they might be exposed to black militant ideas; they knew that the life expectancy of black militants in America is short.

Alumni scattered throughout the South talked about the college, and the school choir annually went on a public relations tour of Southern black high schools. The college coaches actively recruited players throughout the South. With scholarship money, they enticed a few athletes from Chicago's South Side; the Northern blacks, however, were out of place among the timid Southern Negroes and usually didn't stay very long. But from all over the South—Louisiana, Mississippi, Georgia, Tennessee, Florida, Texas—young people came to Thomas, drawn by the promise of a "free" education.

Many were promised scholarships in exchange for their athletic or musical talents, but the scholarship usually proved to be a sales gimmick, like a "free" plastic flower with an expensive box of detergent. Near the end of the year, the business office would discover that the student had used up his scholarship money and owed a large debt to the school. Amazed at the amount of his indebtedness and afraid that he would lose his college credits, the student would gladly sign the paper that the college assured him would "take care of everything"—an application for a loan.

The college also offered a work-study program in which many students participated. Funded by the federal government, which provided $191,600 in 1970, the program paid the college to pay its students for part-time jobs on the campus. Unlike the responsible work-study jobs offered on other campuses, however, most of the jobs at Thomas were menial: kitchen helper, floor sweeper, errand boy. And many of them did not exist at all except on paper. Student workers commonly filled out their own time sheets, signed their supervisor's name, and turned them in to the pay-roll office. In many cases, professors signed falsified time sheets for their "assistants" under the mistaken notion that they were "helping the poor kids" by authorizing pay for nonexistent jobs. But whether the student actually worked for his pay or not, sooner or later he would find that the money didn't go very far. At the end of each pay period, he might get a small check—perhaps five or six dollars if he had worked forty hours. More often, he received a bill indicating that his monthly wage was less than the monthly payment owed to the college.

Many other students received aid from the federal Educational Opportunities Program, which gave Thomas students a total of $203,900 in 1970. A similar state program provided $178,000 for Thomas students during the same year. Yet, no matter what the size of an individual student's grant, the money usually didn't stretch far enough. Sooner or later, most students were compelled to apply for a federal loan under the National Defense Education Act.

Any student whose family income is insufficient to pay his

college expenses can apply for a low-interest loan through
NDEA; loan money is available as long as he is in school, and
he need not begin to repay it until he has graduated. The
program has made it possible for thousands of students across
the country to complete their education, but at Thomas it
was used to enslave them. Thomas students were encouraged
to sign loan applications immediately, and most were forced
to do so eventually because they were refused their grades
and their credits until their bills were paid in full. So year
after year they applied for large loans, saddling themselves
with an indebtedness far out of proportion to the income
they could reasonably expect to earn after graduation. Most
students did not seem to understand what they were
signing, and college officials seldom bothered to explain.
Often students were under the impression that they were
applying for a gift; many had no idea that they were
obligated to pay the money back. Since they thought the
money a gift, few kept track of the amount. Even the few
students who didn't need the money were urged to sign up
for extra funds.

Many students also believed that the money came from
the college rather than from the federal government, and
that Thomas was the only school that had such funds available. Consequently, many students who would have preferred
to transfer to other schools remained tied to Thomas. Thinking that the college provided their funds—or at least that
their support was contingent upon the college—most students
also felt constrained to conduct themselves subserviently, to
humbly accept the indignities heaped upon them by teachers
and administrators rather than risk losing their financial aid.
A student in one of my classes expressed the common view:
"Seemingly the ratio of students to a high degree are either
working their way through or on loans or scholarships. To
keep these funds necessary for getting an education a student
must take dirt thrown in his face because he is poor and

cannot consider another course to take." When they did find out the true nature of the forms they had been signing, it was usually too late. Owing all that money to the government, they could not drop out of school and hope to repay it out of a laborer's wages. Thinking the money contingent upon Thomas College, and not knowing they could continue their loans at any one of the innumerable better colleges, they remained bound to Thomas, "unable" to transfer and in too deep to quit. For this aid to impoverished students the federal government in 1970 lent Thomas students $173,000—or, according to another Thomas report, $198,500.

The management of the student's money, of course, was not left up to him. His account was handled by the college business office. He was charged for his tuition and fees, his dormitory room, and his meals—whether he ate them or not. He had to buy his books and supplies from the "company store," which usually charged inflated prices; and since the store refused to buy back his used textbooks—which other students then could have bought at lower, second-hand prices—he was stuck with them. He was even supposed to send his dirty wash to the campus laundry. The college could have established prices for these "services" as close to cost level as possible. At the very least, the school store could have bought the students' used books and resold them, as most student bookstores do. And the college could have made certain that the student who had paid for his meals did not leave the cafeteria hungry. Instead, it continued to record a neat profit on these enterprises: $219,600 in 1969, $260,000 in 1970.

All these expenses appeared on the student's monthly bill, often accompanied by miscellaneous items for which he could get no explanation. "Most of the time," a student wrote, "we don't really know where all of our money from our loans is going. We have to pay fees in which we have never heard of." The student's monthly statement also included credits accruing from a scholarship, a grant, a work-study job, a loan, or his parents' payment, but the credit list was seldom as long as the debit. Yet few students dared to question the bountiful college for fear that its largesse might cease. Instead, they went on timidly accepting their bills and signing up for loans.

While making the student financially dependent, the college stole from him whatever sense of responsibility and achievement he once may have enjoyed. At Thomas, everything—including student activities—was planned *for* the student. Arrangements for the homecoming festivities, the major event of the year's social calendar, were made by faculty, not student, committees, a college policy that served two purposes, for while students lose self-esteem by having their social events arranged for them by adults, professors also lose self-esteem when compelled to spend hours devising the distribution of crepe paper in the college gymnasium. So little were the students regarded that even the queen of the homecoming was not a student but an alumna, usually one of the secretaries on the administration's staff.

Similarly, the "student" newspaper, which appeared irregularly a few times during the year, was written by a professor and censored by President Greeson; most students didn't bother to read the paper anyway, because it contained only news of the accomplishments of the administration. The college yearbook, too, was composed and assembled by a staff member employed almost exclusively for that task and titled significantly Director of Media and Public Relations. It was not by chance that the yearbook was frequently dedicated to a member of the central administration. Every activity traditionally managed by students at most colleges had been usurped at Thomas by the administration. Members of the student council were elected by students, but since the slate of candidates was formulated in the president's office, few students bothered to vote. The school choir was run by its director, Mr. Hadden. The drama club, at which attendance was required of all who wished to pass speech, was directed firmly by Mrs. Hood. The literature club, which all English majors were required to attend, was lectured week after interminable week by its leader, Dr. Harder. Across the campus there was no student organization in which students had a voice. Even the sororities and fraternities were directed by faculty and administration "big sisters" and "big brothers." Yet at the same time, I numbered among my students one young man who had taken most of the photographs for the yearbook of his Chicago high school, another who had been editor of his high school's weekly newspaper, and another who had designed and supervised all the Christmas decorations for his large high school. These students were justly proud of their skills and achievements, but Thomas had no use for their talents.

In exchange for the student's money and obedience, the college was supposed to provide certain services—housing, food, and the usual auxiliary programs of a college. But the student didn't receive very much for his money.

Recently the college had built some modern dormitories in which students were housed in relative comfort, but most of the students still lived in ramshackle brick and frame buildings, some of them fifty or sixty years old. Three or four students were crowded into each tiny room, in which army-surplus bunks served as beds. With the buildings poorly ventilated in summer and inadequately heated in winter, the students alternately baked in the Southern sun and shivered under a pile of blankets and coats through frozen December nights. Winter winds rattled the flimsy buildings, and in summer the flies swarmed through the unscreened windows. Roaches and scorpions crawled the floors, and sewer rats crept up through the pipes where green fungus spawned on the cracked bathroom walls. There was no place to study, no room for a desk or even a bookshelf in the overcrowded rooms; and besides, there were too many people around to permit concentration. Then, too, the room might be turned inside out at any moment by a matron or a dean, or even occasionally by the local police making a "routine search," for even though the rooms were legally rented by the students, they remained the property of the college. The students had to be reminded of that fact once in a while; let a kid think a room is "his" and there is no telling what other high and mighty notions he might conceive.

The students' meals matched their housing. The cafeteria was run by a very capable woman whom the students adored. She, in return, liked the students and did the best she could for them, but the cafeteria was expected to show a large annual profit. The aim was to fill people as cheaply as possible, so although the food sometimes was quite well prepared, it was starchy and scarce. The largest and best meal of the day was served at noon, when many faculty members ate in the cafeteria. A typical lunch might consist of one small fried fish cake stretched with cereal, fried potatoes, barbecued red beans, corn bread, and a small portion of boiled greens and hot peppers. For dessert there might be a sliver of white cake or a syrupy cobbler made with canned fruit. Fresh fruit and vegetables or an ample portion of real meat, poultry, eggs, or fish were seldom served, and milk never. The beverage was always "punch," a sugary, watered-down Kool-Aid. The evening meal—served in the late afternoon so the kitchen staff could go home early—was scarcely more than a snack. By nine or ten o'clock the students were hungry again. They were, after all, growing teen-agers who needed a lot of nutritious food. Understandably, the most sought-after jobs on campus were those of the cafeteria helpers—because the kitchen workers were allowed to eat the leftovers.

The students often grumbled about the food, the only

aspect of the college they felt reasonably safe in criticizing, but their protests didn't change the menu. After a while the diet betrayed itself as students took on the bloated puffiness that comes with eating too many starches, the layer of fat that masks undernourishment. Nothing was more characteristic of the students than their singular lack of energy, their extraordinary passivity and lethargy. A great many of them were constantly hungry, and many must have been suffering from malnutrition.

Why did the students tolerate these abominable living conditions? The answer was evoked in an English class discussion one day when a young man began complaining because the heat in the dormitories was turned off at night. His classmates pounced on him.

"What make you so special, you gotta have the heat on all night?" a girl demanded. "You never had so much heat before. You ever get all that heat in the day?"

"No," the young man admitted, "but if they goin' to have it in the day they can have it in the night, too. Beside, you feel it more in the night, cuz you wake up with your insides jes' turnin' round and round. If they goin' to turn off the heat, why don't they give you some supper so's you can sleep through it?"

"Lord, you think you be somebody!" a classmate jeered. "When you ever get so much to eat before? Your mama feed you three times in one day?"

"That don't make no difference," the young man countered. "I never paid my mama like I pay here. If I'm goin' pay to eat, I want to eat."

"You might oughta be glad you can eat at all," the girl scolded. "My mama, she be workin' all the time and I never seen so much food before. It's good, too."

"Yeah," others agreed. "Them cobbler things, they is good!"

Most of the students were accustomed to going without

heat and making do with one or two meals a day. Even the rats and the roaches were nothing new. Bad as conditions at the college were, for most students they were better than those at home.

In addition to housing and feeding their students, most colleges commonly make some provision for their leisure time, using part of the students' fees to pay for recreational facilities and cultural events. Thomas, too, provided recreation. There were two pool tables recently installed in a dormitory basement, a small room in the cafeteria building where the kids could play cards or listen to a juke box, and one or two Coke machines. Occasionally, a dance with recorded music was held in the gym, but the admission charge was prohibitive for many students. A few students drove cars, but for most there was no transportation to the movie theaters downtown, and the movies were too expensive anyway. There just wasn't much for a student with time on his hands to do.

The college also provided a series of cultural events, but the programs were so boring that few students bothered to attend. The series included two saccharine student plays, one or two concerts by the school choir, and five sermons by a visiting preacher during Religion Week (when attendance was required). No films, no speakers, no bands. Neighboring black colleges sometimes brought famous personalities to the area—Julian Bond, Ralph Ellison, Shirley Chisholm—but Thomas refused to provide buses so that its students could attend. Once in a while, a student group tried to bring a speaker to campus, but the president refused to have "anything controversial." Without the authority to invite a guest or the money to pay him, the students could do nothing.

Thrown upon their own resources, the students found little to do. When they tired of dormitory bull sessions, they usually went drinking at a near-by club or an off-campus apartment, then climbed into the back of a car. Or they might wander down to the main street of the black district

and provoke a fight with some of the local boys. In consequence, a few young men were knifed or shot, and often
girls were sent home pregnant. But what else were they to
do for "fun"?

The pregnant girls who were deported or bound into
unhappy premature marriages might not have been in that
predicament if the college health service had dealt realisti-
cally with the students' needs. Brought up in strongly religious homes and sheltered by fearful families, most of the
girls desperately needed information about sex and methods
of contraception. They had been taught only that premarital
sex was a sin, and when they discovered that, like so many
sins, it was also pleasurable, they were lost. Away from home
for the first time with nowhere to turn for guidance, they
blundered along until they were caught in a biological trap.
Understanding only that some means of preventing preg-
nancy had to be employed, several girls confiscated from
another young woman in their dormitory a box of vaginal
deodorant suppositories, under the misapprehension that they
were contraceptives. Two of the girls subsequently were sent
home pregnant. But the college assumed no responsibility;
it was easier to deport the girls as morally unfit for a Christian college. The number of pregnancies at Thomas might
have indicated to a concerned administration that its students needed special counsel. Yet Thomas not only declined
to offer such counsel; it interfered with students who had
received instruction at home. When a dormitory matron's
prowling uncovered contraceptive pills in a student's room,
the pills were confiscated and the young woman was lectured
sternly by the outraged dean of women on the subject of
Christian morality. Only a long-distance phone call from an
irate father—who happened to be paying personally all his
daughter's college bills—effected restoration of the young
woman's pills.

The college health service, however, was concerned with
more important matters. The full-time health service con-

sisted of a nurse who dispensed cold tablets and aspirin, took temperatures, and wrote out excuses for students too ill to attend class. When a student was seriously ill, a consulting doctor—a local black physician—was called in, but only after the case had gone through the proper channels. A student who took to his bed had to be visited first by his dormitory matron, an old woman with no particular training. If she thought he really was sick—students were usually accused of malingering—she sent him to the nurse, who treated the patient with aspirin. If the patient did not improve, the nurse reported the case to the president, who decided whether or not the doctor should be called. And if he were called, the doctor decided whether or not he should come. By that time, of course, the patient might be desperately ill. No student really wanted to see the doctor anyway because everyone had heard rumors of his incompetence. They believed that seeing the nurse was useless and that seeing the doctor was tantamount to being placed under sentence of death. So, with all kinds of undiagnosed and untreated ailments, they simply carried on.

Students were equally reluctant to confide their problems to the school counselors, the dean of men, the dean of women, and the dean of student affairs. No one really knew what all those deans and their assistants did, but they didn't appear to do much for the students. Instead, the army of counselors operated as overseers on the plantation, a practice that seems to be common in some black colleges, according to Tilden and Wilbert LeMelle.

The administration of students in the traditional Negro college can best be typified as a form of paternalism, the object of which is to protect and train in a narrow and authoritarian fashion. The result of this form of student administration is student oppression: It inhibits free development, stifles initiative, and frustrates the spirit of intellectual inquiry. On black campuses, deans of students and counselors assume responsibility for students that generally exceeds the solicitousness of very watchful parents. . . . This kind of student administration is totally unwarranted today and has done considerable harm.[1]

At Thomas, the deans and counselors seemed to function mainly as hanging judges, meting out punishment to students accused by dormitory matrons or professors of one infraction or another. Former schoolteachers or ministers, they were untrained as counselors and unfamiliar with the personal and academic life of the students; their official "philosophy" cited as their aim the development in the students of "a Christian attitude to the difficulties of everyday life" and "a cooperative spirit in all aspects of life at Thomas College." A student who shared a personal problem with a counselor would be offered not understanding and practical advice but a moral lecture. Like the faculty, the counselors regarded the students as the enemy whose every move had to be spied out and reported to headquarters. Anything told to a counselor in confidence would soon be repeated in the president's ear. Still, the counselors were held up to the students not only as advisers but as model citizens, worthy of emulation. The deans formally distributed student awards —to the same kids every time—and said prayers and made speeches in daily chapel. Clearly, they were important people, and the students regarded them with a combination of fear and distrust that passed for respect. When the dean of student affairs transformed a lecture entitled "Black Power" into a moralistic sermon on the value of hard work in achieving middle-class status, the students applauded; only a few of the Chicago blacks grimaced in disgust.

Knowing little about the world outside the campus, the counselors could offer students only meager vocational information. They arranged a few job interviews with representatives from factories and black public schools and re-

---

[1] Tilden J. LeMelle and Wilbert J. LeMelle, *The Black College: A Strategy for Achieving Relevancy* (New York: Praeger, 1969), p. 87.

cruiters from the armed forces, giving students the mistaken impression that only the jobs offered were available. About graduate schools, for which some students might have qualified, the counselors knew nothing. Seniors in their last weeks of school announced their "plans" to enter graduate or professional school, not knowing how or where to apply—or that they should have applied months before. Since Thomas admitted anyone who had completed, or nearly completed, high school, the students assumed that they had only to appear at a graduate school, college diploma in hand, to enroll. Their counselors, instead of trying to gather information for them, simply encouraged the fantasies, speaking proudly of the great number of Thomas students who would go on to graduate study this year. The only Thomas student who actually entered a graduate school during the year I spent at the college did so on the strength of Mr. Rogers's advice and recommendation, and over the opposition of the counselors and Dean Butler, who considered the fellow a troublemaker.

Two years before, the young man had been expelled for participating in a mild-mannered student protest against the skimpy cafeteria food, but when he returned to Thomas as a wounded Vietnam veteran, Greeson readmitted him. Although the administrators feared and disliked the student, they wanted his GI Bill money, so at the end of his last semester they unearthed one or two required courses that he had not yet taken. He enrolled for another semester at Thomas and, with Rogers's help, arranged to be admitted to graduate school the following semester. But as graduation time approached again, Butler discovered another required course the student had failed to take, and neither the student nor the college could produce written proof of the fact that a previous dean had exempted the student from the course. Thomas insisted that he enroll for another semester. Mr. Rogers argued that the young man could accomplish much more for himself and for Thomas by becoming the first Thomas graduate to be admitted to the state university graduate school, but Greeson and Butler were adamant. The graduate school faculty, however, had been so impressed by the young man during personal interviews that they cut through the red tape, enabling the student to enter without his undergraduate degree, taking his last required undergraduate course there along with his graduate courses, and transferring the undergraduate credits back to Thomas. Challenged by a stimulating university, he became a very good student, completed his master's degree with an outstanding record, and entered a well-known university for doctoral studies. Although Thomas belatedly claimed the credit for his success, it has still not awarded him an undergraduate degree.

If career counseling was inadequate at Thomas, the academic counseling students received from the deans and their faculty advisers was criminal. Deans and advisers passed on misinformation to the students to keep them on the Thomas account books. One of my freshman students declared that he was majoring in veterinary science, and when I told him that the college did not offer that course of study, he explained that veterinary science was the "same as science." After four years as a science major, he honestly expected to graduate as a full-fledged veterinarian. That is what his adviser had told him. When another student professed to be studying architecture, I explained that the college didn't teach architecture and gave him the names of universities in the region that did, suggesting that he transfer to one of them. Later, thinking that I had misinformed him, he told me rather belligerently that he had decided to stay at Thomas; his adviser had assured him that none of the schools I had listed offered a program as good as Thomas's. Many students talked of their majors in premed, engineering, or computer science—none of which the college offered. Many spoke of being doctors or lawyers when they graduated, not knowing that they had to attend a professional school to earn an additional degree.

Many of the young people who came to Thomas had never had an opportunity to speak with a doctor, a lawyer, an architect, or a veterinarian. How were they to know what went into the education of a professional? And since so many of them were the first in their families to attend college, the maze of undergraduate curricula and requirements presented a world of confusion. They had to trust their advisers and counselors to guide them, but the counselors themselves possessed little of the information the students needed. Defensively, they blundered their way through, unable to admit to the students that they didn't know what they were talking about. Many professors whose acquaintance with the academic world had been gained solely at Thomas probably were sincere in thinking that "veterinary science" and "science" represented the same thing and that "philosophy" was just another name for "religion."

But the most fundamental reason for the existence of Thomas College was—or should have been—to educate its students. Perhaps all else could have been excused if only the school had provided the kids with an education. But at Thomas the business of education had become just a business; education had been forgotten.

The students didn't learn much, and what they were taught was often misleading or simply wrong. But what could they be expected to learn from their obsolete textbooks and archaic courses? All students were required to take one year of freshman English and one year of literature. The program sounded rather old-fashioned on paper, but in practice it proved even more limited. The freshman year was supposed to consist of a semester of grammar and sentence diagraming and a semester of reading aloud from a textbook written by Dr. Harder. In that text, the chapter scheduled to receive greatest emphasis listed and elaborated upon the major faults characteristic of the black masses who purportedly retard the progress of the race. The masses are, for example, characteristically unpunctual. They neglect their property, hold improper values, lack ambition and a sense of responsibility, and speak incorrect English. They are often loud and clownish in public places. They are untidy and poorly groomed; cases have even been recorded of black men sitting on their own front porches in their undershirts. Since most Thomas students represented the black masses, English teachers were required to stress mastery of this crucial chapter. In other words, English teachers were supposed to spend a full semester indoctrinating all the students in the old white racist stereotypes, using as a text a book written by the most "distinguished Negro scholar" on the campus.

Having been taught as freshmen about the shocking behavior of inferior blacks, the students proceeded in the sophomore year to study "great" literature—the accomplishments of the white man. (That some of those great white men happen to have been black was never mentioned, probably because the professors didn't know it.) For one semester, they studied the Greeks and Romans, for another the medieval period. Then the students were officially finished with English, although they had never read a word written since the early Renaissance—except, of course, Dr. Harder's. Students who elected to major in English were required to take courses in English literature (up to the nineteenth century), American literature (up to about 1900), Milton, Shakespeare, and another two semesters of sentence diagraming in courses entitled "The English Language" and "The Grammar of Correct English." They might also elect Dr. Harder's course in "Negro Literature," in which they would read Phillis Wheatley, Booker T. Washington, and, again, Dr. Harder.

Also required of all students was a course entitled "Philosophy," taught by the omnipresent Dr. Harder. In this course, she read aloud to her students another of her books, this one on "man's great thoughts." The text was a compilation of one-line aphorisms culled from philosophers, Shakespeare, the Bible, and Benjamin Franklin. In putting the text together, Dr. Harder had selected bits and pieces out of context to align each of her great philosophers on the side of God, mother, country, and culture. Under Dr. Harder's magic touch, even Karl Marx became an advocate of Christian charity when he wrote "to each according to his needs." As a result, her students emerged from the course with a rather distorted view of the world's great thinkers and a jaundiced opinion of the study of "philosophy."

The English department had no corner on irrelevancy. Home economics students happily learned to cook and sew and keep house while studying to be "fashion designers." Music majors who had been attracted by the instrumental music curriculum advertised in the college catalogue sang in the choir or studied piano while preparing to be "band directors," for, except in the pages of the catalogue, the college offered no program in instrumental music. Business students learned typing and shorthand, thinking that they were being trained to be executives. Perhaps the training the college provided was more realistic than the students' goals, for the would-be fashion designer would probably become a housewife, and the female business students, at least, would become secretaries. But who could say with certainty that among those hopeful young people there was not at least one talented fashion designer, one fine band director, one successful business executive? No one, least of all the students nurturing their precious dreams, would ever know.

The performance of Thomas students on standardized college tests for which national norms have been determined constitutes one measure of the college's success in the business of education. As has been noted, here and elsewhere, national standardized tests are geared to the norms of white middle-class culture and are neither fair nor accurate measures of the abilities of lower-class and black students. The entire educational program at Thomas, however, is designed, not for the special interests of black students, but for the propagation of white middle-class values. Consequently, although entering freshmen may be expected to score very low on standardized tests, more advanced students should earn progressively higher scores if the college is fulfilling its professed educational goals. Unfortunately, that does not seem to be the case. Examining the scores of Thomas students is instructive, for although they do not indicate the students' real abilities, they do illustrate the school's failure.

On one such test, designed to measure the level of general knowledge college students have acquired during the first two college years, Thomas students indicated that they had acquired very little. In social science, seventy-one of the seventy-five students tested near the end of their sophomore year scored between the fourth and the sixteenth national percentiles. In other words, between 84 and 96 per cent of college sophomores throughout the country performed better than the Thomas students. In the area of humanities, fifty-eight of the Thomas sophomores ranked between the fourth and the sixteenth percentiles; in mathematics, sixty-eight; in natural science, seventy-three; and in English, sixty-nine. Moreover, in natural science, eighteen of the seventy-five students ranked below the second percentile, while in English thirty-seven students fell into that abysmal category. Only two students scored above the fiftieth percentile on any portion of the test, one in English and one in humanities, but such anomalies are more reasonably attributed to the individual student's background than to his Thomas education.

Another national test administered to seniors graduating

with degrees in education was designed to measure the student's general knowledge, his knowledge in the specific field he had prepared to teach, and his "professional" knowledge or acquaintance with the theories and practice of education. Of the twenty-three Thomas students tested, twelve of them ranked at the fourth percentile or below on the general education section of the test; four of these students fell within the first percentile. On this segment of the test, only four students ranked higher than the tenth percentile and only one of them higher than the sixteenth. On the portion of the test that assesses a student's familiarity with the subject he plans to teach, thirteen of the twenty-three Thomas seniors ranked at or below the fourth national percentile, five of them at or below the first percentile. Seven of the students, or about one-third, ranked above the tenth percentile, but only two of them scored above the seventeenth percentile. The over-all composite scores on the test rated twenty-two of the twenty-three students below the fifteenth percentile, nineteen of them below the tenth percentile, sixteen of them (or more than two-thirds) below the fifth percentile. The test figures indicate that the Thomas education graduates, with one exception, were less well prepared than 85 per cent of education graduates throughout the country and that two-thirds of them were less well educated than 95 per cent of students across the country who had studied for the same degree. The single Thomas student who achieved a respectable score, a young woman who finished in the seventy-second percentile on her composite score, clearly was another anomaly, probably owing more to her background than to Thomas.

These education majors, whose deplorable scores reflect the quality of their Thomas education, comprised a little less than one-half of their graduating class. If any standardized test was administered to the graduating seniors who majored in a field other than education, the test results were not furnished to the faculty; but the performance of the education majors is probably a little better than that of the other students, for the education major is the college's strong suit.

As I have noted, most of the students admitted to Thomas as freshmen have only the most rudimentary educational background. From the outset, they are deficient. A standardized test given the freshmen a few years ago, however, indicated that they compared to national norms more favorably than did the seniors. The test measured background in four areas—English, mathematics, social science, and natural science—and yielded a composite score that might be compared with national norms for freshmen just entering college. Unfortunately, the test results were tabulated for only 160 of the 213 Thomas freshmen who took the test. (That the results were not compiled for all the tested students seems strange, but half-hearted effort is a Thomas tradition.) For those students, the composite scores were predictably low; almost one-third ranked below the twentieth national percentile, two-fifths below the tenth. On the other hand, almost one-fifth of the tabulated freshmen scored between the twenty-fourth and forty-ninth percentiles, and almost one-eighth ranked above the fiftieth percentile. Eight students placed above the seventy-fifth percentile, a high ranking that does not appear among the seniors' test scores. Even allowing for the fact that one group of students may be superior to another by sheer chance, it would seem that the Thomas freshmen are not so hopeless as the college would like to think. It would also seem that after four years of teaching its "special type of student" the college might reasonably be expected to produce better senior test scores.

Thomas, to my knowledge, has never conducted a thorough study of the performance of its students, but these fragmentary scores seem to indicate that Thomas students progress steadily backward. One explanation, of course, is that brighter students tend to leave Thomas; either they transfer out or they are expelled for various forms of insubordination. Brighter slaves find a means of delivering themselves from bondage, while the duller perform the assigned chores and are rewarded with diplomas. Whether that theory is adequate to explain the downhill slide of Thomas students must remain a moot question until the college undertakes a study of its own students. In any case, the explanation does little credit to the school. Nevertheless, the state and federal governments, which require no records of student achievement, continue to provide hundreds of thousands of dollars each year to keep Thomas in the business of education. And the graduates it has "educated"—all those first-percentile seniors—continue to find teaching jobs in the predominantly black public schools of the South.

Another explanation for the backward progress of the students lies in the brainwashing they receive. Schooled by texts like Dr. Harder's to regard blacks as inferior, they are treated every day as though they themselves are the worst of the niggers. Their teachers boss them around, laugh at them, assign them meaningless tasks, and speak openly of their stupidity. Youngsters who arrive on the campus happy and eager to learn become lethargic within a few weeks or months. The students' records commonly show the same pattern: a semester or two of A grades followed by a more or less sudden drop. By junior year, students who began school with straight A's are receiving low D's and F's. Characteristically, they become passive, lazy, completely disinterested in things around them. Many quit attending classes altogether and finally flunk out; others drag through to graduation. The reason is simple: they are behaving as they are expected to behave—according to the racist stereotype of the dumb, lazy nigger.

Another reason for their disinterest is that there is so

little to be interested in. The classes usually are boring, and the students aren't expected to participate anyway. If they read the lessons before class, the boredom is intensified, for the teacher repeats what they have already read. If they do the assignments well, the teacher will accuse them of cheating. If they do them badly, the teacher will bawl them out. If they ask questions, the teacher will humiliate them. The safest policy, and the easiest, is to do nothing.

Under such treatment, less timid students become hostile and rebellious. Since they cannot risk expulsion by openly defying the teacher, they develop an elaborate set of defensive mechanisms. They come late to class—or not at all. They forget to read the books or do the assignments. They come to class without pen and paper, and since they obviously cannot take notes, they fall asleep, or pretend to. They refuse to speak up in class and turn in blank examination papers. Somewhere inside them is the sense that other people—even teachers—do not have the right to treat them as they do. But since the feeling cannot be voiced (it is usually not even a conscious thought), they express it in the only way they know. The teacher's behavior says to them: "You are too stupid to learn anything." And the students respond tacitly: "You can't teach me anything." Whether the students are frightened, bored, or hostile, the results are the same. They do not learn.

Education at Thomas was a failure, but the brainwashing was eminently successful because it reinforced lessons the students had already been taught by the public schools and their life in a segregated society. The freshman boys came to school willing and eager to "get educated" so they could "get better jobs." The girls, less ambitious, hoped to be married eventually to men who had "high-class jobs." They were eager, in other words, to escape the life they had known, a life in which they were doubly oppressed as blacks and as poor people, a life in which they were as nothing.

There is nothing dishonorable in the desire to raise one's position, but, to them, achieving status also meant gaining identity. Subject for so long to the judgments of the white world, they had accepted the standards of others as their own. Now they judged themselves by those standards and pronounced themselves worthless, inferior. Yet they had not been completely destroyed. They had not accepted the lot assigned them at birth. Although they thought of themselves as poor, dumb "colored," they were determined not to remain so. In their ambition lay the last vestiges of perverted pride: not an inner sense of their own value, but a desperate longing to justify their existence by accumulating tangible evidence—a college degree, a big car, a fancy house, money to spend. They were dreamers of the American dream.

They knew little about their cultural past and even less about the present. Of course, they idolized Booker T. Washington and Martin Luther King, Jr., but my freshmen had never heard of Malcolm X, and the few who had heard of Stokely Carmichael knew only that he was a "godless Communist." Of Richard Wright, Ralph Ellison, James Baldwin, Imamu Baraka, Huey Newton, Eldridge Cleaver, Angela Davis, and countless others, they knew nothing. To remedy the situation, Dr. Norden and I opened a lending library with a bookshelf stacked with "black" books. A few students began to read avidly, but most, unwilling to confront their own negritude, conscientiously avoided the books. Others took offense at language they had never before seen in print and had been taught to consider ill bred if not downright sinful. One young woman ceremoniously tore up and flushed down the toilet my copy of Baldwin's *Blues for Mr. Charlie,* probably to express her hostility toward me, but ostensibly to express her disgust with the play's "dirty language."

To interest a broader group of students, I gave my classes Eldridge Cleaver's *Soul on Ice,* only to discover when we began to talk about the book that I had made a monstrous mistake. Totally unprepared to confront the issues Cleaver discusses, yet troubled by the echoes in their own experience, most of the students had to erect some defense against the book. The morally upright dismissed Cleaver as a "jailbird"; those who were troubled by his discussion of sex found him "dirty-minded." Others noted his opposition to black participation in the Vietnam war and denounced him as a "Communist fascist." But the most unexpected and the most common verdict pronounced Cleaver an Uncle Tom. They reasoned that Cleaver must be writing what whites wanted to hear since his book had been recommended by a white teacher, while the older black teachers of whom they inquired had never heard of him.

Yet a few students "turned on" to Cleaver, reading and rereading his book, puzzling over it in night-long bull sessions, asking to borrow other books like "Brother Cleaver's." And one young man, who had never before written a complete English sentence, proudly showed me the inscription he had written in the front of *Soul on Ice*: "This is *my* book. Keep your fucking hands off." And he had signed his full name with a flourish.

The students who reacted so defensively to Cleaver had been whitewashed from their earliest years. But that they had come to college at all indicated that they were not wholly complacent, not completely resigned to keeping their place. Thomas might have given them some information about their own heritage and some understanding of the world in which they lived. Barring such "controversial" material, the college could have treated them with respect, conveying to them some sense of their own worth. Instead, it applied more whitewash and ruthlessly "put the niggers in their place."

At the same time, black professors and administrators told tall tales about the deference paid to them by "high-class" whites and how they had put "low-class" whites in their place. The stories usually concerned a favor the black had done for a white "friend," usually some important person in the community, or the way the black had said to the white worker at the car wash, "Boy, you better make that Cadillac shine!" The fantasies on the old racist lines, but with the racial roles reversed, provided favorite and frequent topics of conversation. The students listened with awe and admiration, believing every word and learning well the subtle lesson: that the value of a man lies in his money and position, not in the integrity of the self. They learned, too, that when they gained the money and position of the middle class, they in turn could look down on the low-class niggers, both black and white.

Another favorite topic of faculty monologues was "What a Great Man I would have become had I been white." Professors talked of having been offered the highest positions in academic life, the arts, politics, only to have the offers withdrawn when their race was discovered. Many of the stories undoubtedly contained some truth, for equal opportunity in America remains a myth. But many of the stories were the excuses of men who had never ventured greatly. The pernicious tales were picked up by the students to justify their own fears of the racist world. The case of one talented senior was typical. He talked incessantly of his feverish ambition to study radio and television in graduate school. He was already an experienced radio announcer, and, with graduate training, he thought he could advance rapidly. Eventually he hoped to own his own television station, and he was already mapping out the new programs he would produce. One of his teachers had gathered information and application forms for the young man, and I wrote to a friend who headed a communications department at a well-known university. My friend responded that his department would be happy to accept the young man and offered such generous scholarships to blacks that money would be no obstacle. I turned over the application forms I had received to the student, but he never filled them out; nor did he apply to any of the universities his other teacher had contacted. Months later, a friend in the community reported to me what the young man had told him: that he could not go to graduate school because none of the schools to which he had applied accepted blacks.

Side by side with this fantasy, complementing it, marched the pervasive belief that life is miraculously easy for white people. Many students who visited Dr. Dexter were amazed to find her sewing shirts or patching blue jeans for her teen-aged son. When she explained that she could not afford to buy new clothes at the rate her son wore them out, the students were shocked. Even a professor, finding Dr. Dexter at her sewing, exclaimed, "I didn't know white folks sewed!" That a white woman should perform the same tasks as a black woman was, to them, unthinkable. Similarly, a young man in one of my classes angrily accused me of holding a job that some black needed. "You're rich," he declared. "You don't need a job." He was reluctant to believe that I, too, had to earn an income. When I explained that I had earned part of my own college expenses by working as a waitress and a housemaid, he was convinced that I was lying. "Those jobs," he asserted, "are nigger jobs. No white person would do them." He himself, he told me, had not held a job in the twenty-three years of his life, and he didn't plan to accept one until he was offered a "real white man's job." The Thomas students had to wander only a few blocks from the campus to find white families as poor as their own, yet the myth persisted: all white people are rich. And in a sense, of course, compared to the oppressed blacks, they are.

Thus, for many youngsters, fantasy became a way of life. Like all other people—of every color—they feared failing. Most people find it safer not to risk themselves; they will never achieve their dreams, but at least they can preserve them. As long as they do not put themselves to the test, they cannot fail, and in old age they can still talk of what might have been. For black people, who have been systematically trained to fear the white world, the temptation to quiescence must be enormous, and they have a convenient, built-in excuse: they are black, and the whole white world conspires to keep them in their place. To defy is dangerous, and to resign is not cowardly so long as one can blame it on someone else.

The college could have given its students the means and the support to overcome their fears. It could have given them the self-respect they needed to take a chance in the world. Instead, it treated them like irresponsible children and instilled in them a pervasive fear of the outside world. For days before the national Vietnam Moratorium Day, one of the most "militant" young men on campus—one of the few who opposed the war—threatened to do "something this town will never forget." When the day came for his grand gesture, he sneaked downtown at four o'clock in the morning to tack a peace poster on the side of the post office; he had wanted to put it on the front door but thought the risk of detection too great. And when I put a peace poster on the door of my office, he advised me in a hoarse whisper to take it down because "they" wouldn't like it.

"Who," I asked him, "are 'they'?"

"Well, I don't exactly know," he said, "but they're watching all the time."

In many cases, the fear of the outside world became so overpowering that students could not leave the college environment. Safe in the womb, they feared the cutting of the cord. They tried, usually without knowing what they were doing, to avoid graduating. One young man contrived several times during the last week of a semester to break a rule for which he would be temporarily suspended, losing his credits for the semester and being "forced" to come back again. Another man, no longer very young, had postponed his graduation for several semesters by neglecting to take certain required courses. Now, taking the last of them and scheduled for graduation in a few days, he suddenly managed to fail a course by oversleeping on the day of the exam. The professor, knowing that the student had to pass the course to graduate, scheduled a make-up exam for him, but again he overslept. A third exam was arranged for an afternoon hour so the fellow could be sure of getting up on time, but on that afternoon he lay down for a nap and again slept through the exam. The professor gave up, for it was clear to him—though not to the student—that the student did not want to pass. So he will be back in school next year and, if he can manage it, the year after that. The college, wanting to keep as many students as possible on the account books, often "finds" that students who are supposed to graduate need one more required course. Not infrequently, students who have just graduated are told that their degree was conferred in error and they must return for one more course. The students complain bitterly about the inefficiency of the college records office, grateful all the while for the chance to remain in the sweet, safe world where their place is so clearly defined for them.

Significantly, it is often the students who outwardly are most militant and hostile who use Thomas as a safe home base. By becoming involved in a fight, insulting the "wrong" teacher or administrator, or cutting an important exam, they precipitate disciplinary action and assure themselves of at least one more semester in college. Among their peers, such students enjoy an enviable reputation as people who are so exuberant and self-assured that they cannot avoid "messing up." One young man who had gained two extra years at Thomas through the game of messing up was famous among the students for his repeated boast: "When I get outta

here, I'm goin' to send ol' Greeson an all-day sucker." Had
he known of the brag, of course, Greeson would have had
every reason to send the student a sucker.

In addition to messing up, the students devised many
other means of adapting to the college environment. One
of the most common was simple withdrawal. After a freshman girl, Areatha, had spent a lively and articulate semester
in my English class, I was surprised by her behavior during
the second semester; although she never missed a class, she
sat through each session in silence, a stony, impassive ex-
pression on her face. Knowing that she was by nature argumentative and vivacious, I asked her the reason for her
silence.

"Do you find the class boring, Areatha?" I inquired.

"No," she replied sullenly.

"Have the other students done something to annoy you?"
I asked. "Have I offended you in any way?"

"No," she answered grimly, "none of that."

When I persisted in my questioning, she finally burst
out angrily, "My mama told me to speak up in school,
and I always did. And when I came here I spoke up for a
whole semester. You know in your class I always spoke up
what I thought. But all my teachers, they just laughed and
laughed at me. My friend Essie, she said to me, 'Areatha,
when you goin' learn to keep your mouth shut?' And I kept
my mouth shut ever since. You never did laugh at me—
I'll give you that much—but if I speak up in your class I'll
forget and speak up in the rest of them. I'll do all the work
the teachers give me, but there ain't no way I'm goin' open
my mouth in class for the next three and a half years."

Areatha was as determined as she was argumentative, so
for the rest of the semester she, and some of her classmates,
sat through classes without ever uttering a sound. For many
naturally passive students, withdrawal provided a convenient
adaptation, but for Areatha, bright and highly articulate,

silent withdrawal required a tremendous exertion of the will. That she could maintain silence was a measure of her strength of character; that she felt she must was an indictment of the college.

A few students, particularly those who came from large cities and had seen more of the world than their rural classmates, endured life at the college by building a counterstructure, a life of their own. Several couples married and moved off the campus to establish homes in the run-down bungalows of the surrounding black residential area, and their homes immediately became off-campus social centers for their student friends. The few young men from Northern cities, whose manner, attitudes, and speech seemed odd and suspicious to the Southern blacks, usually were ostracized on campus, and soon they, too, moved in pairs or small groups to apartments or bungalows in the black community. The removal of the urban and Northern blacks left the campus almost exclusively to the rural and small-town Southern blacks, effectively isolating them from knowledge they might have gained by living with the more worldly-wise students.

Often, of course, the counterstructure a student had built for his survival became more important to him than the college; the longer he stayed at Thomas, the more he hated it, and the more he pursued the life he had fabricated for himself apart from the school. Yet that life, too, was seldom a life he really wanted; he had not freely created it but had chosen it as the lesser of two evils, as a means of avoiding the college. Nevertheless, the young men and the married couples appeared on campus less and less frequently; they came only to attend a few classes now and then, but finally many of them gave up their classes too. They disappeared altogether, many of the young men into menial jobs in the community, earning some money to go back home. The married women became pregnant and dropped out of school to concentrate on homemaking. Their husbands went to work in local factories to pay the bills, and finally—because it is hard to work all night and get up for class in the morning—they, too, dropped out. Some of the couples still talk of going back to school—at a different college—as soon as they can scrape the money together, but in the meantime the young men continue to labor in the factories, the young women in the home. In trying to survive at Thomas they have stumbled into the very blue-collar life they entered college to avoid.

Instead of building a life in opposition to the college, many students take on the life prescribed by the college as their own. Its values become their values, its philosophy their philosophy, its officials their heroes. They are the first to open the door for Mrs. Hood, the first to thank Dr. Harder for a stimulating grammar lesson, the first to congratulate Dean Butler on the brilliance of his latest plan. They sing in the choir, perform in all the plays, and are nominated by the administration to fill seats on the impotent student council. With administration support, they become the official leaders of the student body, giving inspirational talks and prayers in chapel in emulation of their mentors, the college deans. Being so interested in the welfare of the college, they quickly advise the dean of student affairs of any grumbling among the students, identifying "trouble-makers" for the dean to summon for "help" with their "psychological problems." In return for such cooperation, the dean appoints the student leaders to serve on the disciplinary committee to endorse the dean's punishment of their fellow students. Despite their heavy responsibilities, the student leaders earn straight A's in their courses and are appointed to all the honor societies. They constitute the *Who's Who* of Thomas College. Some of them aspire to be college presidents, and a few may reach that goal. Some of the students genuinely admire their leaders, although many call them "Toms."

Most students, however, pass no judgments upon their leaders or upon the college. Since they have never known any other college, they believe that Thomas is a good, representative school, that life at Thomas is similar to college life everywhere. Since Thomas offers them a "great opportunity" for college education, they have swallowed their initial disappointment and resigned themselves to doing as they are told. To the mass of Thomas students their student leaders are awesome and powerful, the urban and Northern blacks different and frightening. The circumspect student takes a middle course, following orders and taking no risks, perhaps remembering the survival technique of his spiritual ancestor: "Br'er Rabbit, he lay low."

There is good reason to lie low at Thomas. Since the college is a closed community within which a small number of administrators and teachers must maintain control of a large number of potentially threatening students, the officials will take "whatever steps are necessary" to ensure "cooperation." For their own security, the college officials must discourage pride, self-confidence, initiative, individuality, independence of thought and action—any form of assertiveness. They must reward obedience, passivity, and lethargy. Most important, they must divide the students from each other and isolate them from their natural leaders.

To divide the students and engender prejudice and animosity among them, the college vigorously supports fraternities and sororities, urging them to vie with one another in supposedly friendly competition. Although the fraternal groups at Thomas are strictly social clubs rather than residential units or service organizations, they consume the largest part of the students' time. All the students spend endless hours rehearsing songs and skits to perform on the grounds during the noon hour, and the girls squander much more money than they can afford on material to sew identical dresses in the colors of their organization. For days before major social events, such as home-coming or a big dance, classrooms are almost deserted as students, excused by the dean of student affairs—himself a fraternity man—decorate their fraternity's float or portion of the gym under the direction of faculty advisers. Students who don't have enough to eat still manage to scrape up the money for a bejeweled fraternity pin. So intense is their devotion to the fraternal system, their only source of worldly status, that some young men carve the Greek initials of their organization with a pocket knife into their own flesh; if the wounds are deep enough, the scars form ropy welts, leaving an upraised insignia on the skin. This devotion, however, is shown not to all fellow students, but only to the system itself and to one's own fraternity brothers and sorority sisters—including administrators and professors. Black faculty members and administrators align themselves with the group to which they belonged as students, wearing their old college pins and exchanging secret handshakes and mumbo jumbo with their student "brothers" and "sisters." The fierce rivalry permeates the college. Thus, whenever a sizable portion of the student body threatens to unite on a campus issue, a well-placed word or two from a "big brother" usually is enough to make the coalition fall apart along fraternity lines.

Once during the year, after the informal visit of two Northern blacks who told of leading a successful drive to institute black studies at their Midwestern university, the Thomas College students were inspired to protest. After a long meeting—which they allowed the dean of student affairs to "chaperon"—the students drew up a list of pathetic "requests" for more heat, more food, and better classes. The young men also humbly asked that the faculty not address them as "boy." Finally, President Greeson "dropped in" to explain to the students in his fatherly way that the college was already working hard on this point or that, and one by one the requests were relinquished. Only on a single point did a small group of girls hold out, but since they represented a lesser sorority, the other students refused to support them, and the issue was dropped. They had wanted some beauty-parlor equipment in the dormitory so they could more conveniently press their hair.

With the student body so well divided, the administration seldom has to act directly against the leaders or potential leaders of student insurrections. Once a natural leader has seen his followers hastily desert his cause, leaving him on the field of battle to face the big guns alone, he is not apt to assume leadership again. If he should persist in rebellion, however, he can be flunked out by cooperative teachers. If prompt action seems required, the administration can simply expel the troublesome student without explanation, but it prefers to press a charge against him so there will be no question of refunding any of his money. Meanwhile, the administration identifies and supports its own student leaders, those loyal retainers who can be exhibited to visiting dignitaries but who would never, never lead the students anywhere.

So effective are the administration's methods that only once in recent memory have the students actually staged a protest. A large number of students boycotted and picketed the cafeteria, demanding more and better food. Unfortunately, the strikers grew hungry and one by one lay down their picket signs to go inside for a meal. The strike dissipated itself while the cafeteria remained the same. Although the students clearly had lost, their momentary unity frightened the administration into action—not to improve the cafeteria, but to punish the demonstrators. The dean of student affairs privately reprimanded each demonstrator, demanding that he give his solemn promise never to disobey again; each student's confession of guilt and vow of obedience was tape-recorded to be used against him in any future disciplinary action. Those students who could not or would not swear perfect obedience into the tape recorder were summarily expelled—some fifty students in all. Under normal circumstances, however, only a few students are expelled each semester.

The expelled students constitute only a fraction of the large number of students who annually leave Thomas. In fact, the annual turnover rate—apart from those who graduate normally—is at least one-third of the student body. The turnover includes those who flunk out, quit, are expelled as troublemakers, or are sent home pregnant; and it is an enormous rate for a small school where students supposedly receive individual attention. The rate of turnover is impossible to determine precisely, for although the college submits to HEW the required figures on student attrition, it submits a different set of figures each year. In both its 1969 and 1970 federal reports, the college was required to list attrition rates for the years 1966 through 1968; the two sets of figures, covering the same period, should, of course, be identical, but in fact they are almost totally different. The 1969 report, for example, says that in 1966, 116 of 123 seniors completed the school year, but the number of graduates is listed as 67. On the other hand, the 1970 report says that only 49 of 109 seniors completed the year in 1966, but it agrees that 67 students graduated. These and other discrepancies are not minor deviations that might be explained by the college's greater accuracy in checking its records for the second time; the divergence between the two reports is enormous. Thus, the 1969 report contends that a total of 393 students completed the 1967 school year, but the 1970 report concedes that only 286 students did— a difference of 107. With fewer than 500 students to account for, the college might reasonably be expected to be more accurate, but it apparently cannot even keep track of the number of students who enroll; the 1969 report says 455 students enrolled in 1967, but the 1970 report puts the figure at 503.

Accuracy and completeness in record keeping, however, seem not to be required by the federal bureau that supports Thomas. When I confronted the officer in charge of the Thomas file with these vast discrepancies, he wrote to Dean Butler requesting clarification. Months later, he sent me Butler's explanation: the figures given in the 1969 report for 1968 refer to the academic year 1967–68, while the figures given in the 1970 report for 1968 refer to the academic year 1968–69. The HEW officer seemed to consider that explanation reasonable and sufficient, and the matter was closed even though the college—knowing that a partial truth is better than the whole—had offered no "clarification" of its divergent figures for 1966 and 1967.

Arbitrarily accepting the more recent figures as the more exact, however, one can trace a single class through its four-year career at Thomas. According to the 1970 report, then, 174 students enrolled as freshmen in 1966 and 108 of them, less than two-thirds of the class, completed the year. In 1967, 121 students began their sophomore year, and 80 of them, about two-thirds, finished. At the beginning of the junior year, in 1968, the class had grown to 102, and 80 of those students, more than three-fourths, completed the year. The 1971 report, which lists the figures for 1969, the year when these students should have been seniors, recorded 17 new transfer students, but the senior class had miraculously expanded from 80 to 132 students. Of this group, 118, or 90 per cent, completed the year, yet strangely enough only 69 students were awarded diplomas.

And the official attrition figures, with all their obvious errors, list only the number of students who begin and complete each year, not the number of students who complete several successive years at the college. The fact that eighty students complete one year at Thomas and eighty the next does not mean that the groups are comprised of the same eighty students. Neither the college nor the federal bureau that supports it keeps a record of the number of students who enter as freshmen and graduate as seniors. To receive its federal grant each year, the college needs a few hundred students, but whether those students continue, advancing steadily toward a degree, or are replaced annually by a new batch makes no difference to the college or the federal government. Providing the guidance, counseling, and tutorial help that Thomas students desperately need to complete their undergraduate education would cost the college a great deal of money. It is easier and less expensive to let the students come and go.

Those students who, for one reason or another, leave the college are probably better off for having done so. The students who remain for a few years usually are devastated by the experience. A sophomore expressed a feeling common among the students: "Students at [Thomas] seem to possess a fear of an inevitable power or a great force against their own will. Truthfully I admit the situation on campus is so absurd in every aspect that it even makes me feel as I was part of a junked-up place, in which there is no way out of the senseless torture." Although I witnessed the students' defeat at every turn, I did not realize the full extent of their whitewashing until I became involved in a heated campus uproar. One day in class, apropos of something we were reading at the time, I mentioned the hypothesis of some biblical scholars that Jesus was black. The story was repeated with anger and astonishment all over campus, and even when my statement was corroborated by the visiting chaplain—a radical black clergyman who had been hired by accident—the gossip continued unabated. I was denounced with every bad name the students could think of—honky, racist, fascist, Communist, pig, hippie—and all because I had suggested the possibility that their

Saviour might have been the same color as themselves. Their God would always be white.

Those students who do well after their education and their whitewashing do so in spite of Thomas College. They are, by any standards, remarkable people. But most of the students who attend Thomas probably will have smaller lives because of the experience; it has given them mainly four or five more years of intensive training in being slaves. They fervently believe that the second greatest modern black man—after Martin Luther King, Jr.—is Simon L. Greeson, and if they can afford the trip, they will return to the old campus on alumni day year after year to celebrate Greeson and their alma mater. Some few students who can live neither in fantasy nor resignation will be destroyed by bitterness and rage, sensing their oppression but unable to identify the anonymous oppressor. And occasionally one of the embittered will do as one of the recent graduates did— go back to his hometown and shoot a cop. And the cop will die for the sins of Simon L. Greeson, and of us all.

7

The Carpetbaggers

Administrators, faculty, and students at Thomas were locked into a dance that could have gone on and on, if only the accrediting board hadn't tried to cut in. Officially, accreditation was "our goal" at Thomas, the goal "in which we all strive," as President Greeson so often said. Unofficially, it was a great deal of trouble.

Many years before, under the aggressive leadership of the indefatigable President Stonewall, the college had been accredited. In those better years, the college must have graduated many young men and women who went on to become doctors, lawyers, ministers, professors, teachers, and businessmen across the Southern black belt. The college must have had some good black faculty members, mainly because at that time black professors were largely confined to teaching in black schools. It must have had many bright students because most black students too were confined to black schools, and there simply were not enough black colleges to accommodate all the students who might have filled them. But even at that time, Thomas was not a first-rate school. It did not have to be, for the proponents of "separate but equal" education have always been willing to be a little lenient about the "equal" as long as the "separate" was rigidly enforced.

President Stonewall's benevolent dictatorship depended ultimately upon the dominant personality of President Stonewall, and when his long reign ended with his death, there was no one to take his place. A series of short-term presidents sent the college into decline, while the best black teachers were wooed away by the better black schools and, increasingly, by Northern universities. As more loans and scholarships became available, and as formerly all-white schools opened their doors to blacks, Thomas could not recruit many excellent students and scarcely even tried. With professors finding better positions and students a much better education elsewhere, there was no reason for Thomas to continue. It had served its purpose during the long period of segregated education; with pride in that accomplishment, it could now close its doors.

But it didn't close. Instead, it took whatever students would still agree to come. Whatever standards the school may have had were forgotten in the effort to get somebody —anybody—to fill the empty spaces in the dormitories. After all, the more students the college enrolled, the more money it could wheedle from the government and philanthropic foundations. Since the new students weren't considered to be very bright, the college didn't need a first-class faculty; it could make do with second- and third-raters and pay them lower salaries. That slapdash system worked until the accrediting board came around, as it does once every ten years, for a checkup. The board completed its routine investigation and hastily withdrew the college's accreditation; the precise date of this disaster remains "classified," shrouded in mystery like the latest missile design.

Accreditation, the official recognition by an association of educators that a college maintains standards that qualify its

graduates for admission to higher institutions or certain professional practices, is essential for all colleges; without this
formal approval, they can hardly expect to attract capable
students and faculty. Few students will choose to work four
years for a degree that will not be acknowledged by graduate
and professional schools or by state teacher certification
agencies; few professors will elect to teach at an unaccredited
college, considering the school's low standards a detrimental
reflection upon their own career credentials. Financially
marginal institutions like Thomas, moreover, depend for
their very lives upon accreditation, for unaccredited schools
are ineligible for most federal and state educational funds.

When Thomas lost its accreditation, the United Negro
College Fund automatically withdrew its financial support.
Private foundations continued to donate money to Thomas
for library improvement, faculty travel, and administrative
reform, but these funds were proffered to help the college
regain its accredited status; they could be cut off if the college did not soon produce evidence of self-improvement.
Worst of all, loss of accreditation put federal Title III funds
beyond reach. To be eligible for HEW grants distributed
under Title III of the Higher Education Act of 1965, a
college is supposed to be at least an officially designated
correspondent of a regional Association of Colleges and
Schools, actively in correspondence with the association, and
working, under its direction, toward accreditation and full
membership. Somehow, although Thomas was not even a
correspondent, it had managed for three successive years to
evade the requirement and had finagled generous grants
from HEW: $64,000, $39,000, and $75,000. When the re-
gional association finally granted Thomas the status of correspondent, Greeson and Baggett must have felt the relief of
the drinker at the repeal of Prohibition; what they had been
doing all along was now, at last, legal. The following year,
they could accept a grant of $86,000 without the slightest

twinge of conscience. The college's correspondent status, however, was only temporary; if Thomas failed to gain accreditation at the next inspection, it would lose its correspondent's rank and fall back to its previous ignominious position.

Another crucial source of income for the college was, as I have noted, the money provided to students through the National Defense Education Act, for although the money was lent by the federal government to the individual student, who was responsible for paying it back, it was handled by the college and could be used pretty much as the administrators saw fit. Most of the students at Thomas were preparing to be elementary or high school teachers. To gain teaching positions, the students had to obtain not only a college degree but a certificate from the state Board of Teacher Certification indicating that they were qualified to teach in the public schools of the state. Unfortunately for Thomas, the teacher certification board would certify only graduates of accredited colleges. The board had been lenient with Thomas, giving it a few years of grace to regain its accreditation and in the meantime examining its graduates individually, certifying some and rejecting others. Now the grace period was coming to an end; if Thomas failed to gain accreditation during the next year, the state board would certify no more of its graduates as teachers and NDEA would provide no more loans to Thomas students who were studying to be teachers.

Aware of the impending crisis, the board of trustees had hired a new president several years before I came to the college. Simon L. Greeson rashly promised to regain accreditation, but when the representatives of the accrediting board visited the campus a year later, he had done nothing. Apparently Greeson didn't know where to begin. So the board sent out its team of consultants, professors and administrators from accredited colleges, to outline for Thomas the changes it had to make. The consultants' reports were long, thorough, detailed, and generally disregarded.

The next step for Thomas was self-study, a project that consumed most of the spring semester the year before I came to the college. During that semester, each department was supposed to study the report of its consultant, revise itself according to the recommendations, and write up a report of the improvements it had made. It was the preliminary result of this self-study that was reported by the department chairmen in the unintelligible speeches I heard during the faculty orientation conference. From the evasions and rationalizations of those preliminary reports, I gathered that the real aim of the self-study was not improvement but self-justification. Typically, the insecure Thomas faculty had taken professional recommendations as personal insults and tried to save face, as they did with the students, by pointing out the incompetence and ignorance of their critics.

During my first semester at Thomas, the self-study, begun almost a year before, was scheduled for completion. The reports of the various departments were to be compiled, edited, transcribed in a uniform prose style, printed, bound, and submitted to the accreditation board. This task had been assigned to the newly arrived Dean Butler, but it proved too much for him. Within a few days, he summoned Dr. Norden and me, asking frantically if we, as English teachers, would help him with the task of editing. We, too, were newcomers and eager to be helpful; without knowing what we were getting into, we agreed. With a few exceptions the department chairmen had taken the occasion of composing their self-study reports to display their most flamboyant rhetoric, often unsupported by recognizable English syntax. Several of the reports were wildly abstract statements of the writer's philosophy of education or, worse, his view of the cosmos. One or two reports had to be returned to the writer because they were incomprehensible; there was simply no way to translate their florid phrases into English. Very few said anything of substance, and only rarely did they address themselves to the recommendations with which they were supposed to deal.

Those that did were often remarkable in their interpretation of the recommendations. The consultant to the English department had stated tactfully but specifically that the English professors were too old and that Dr. Harder in particular was too old-fashioned to retain her powerful positions as chairman of both the English department and the School of Arts and Letters. Undeterred, Dr. Harder herself wrote the self-study report for the English department, stating flatly that the consultant's recommendation had been fulfilled by the hiring of two younger faculty members. She had ignored the point of the consultant's suggestion, presumably reasoning that if the two new recruits were in their thirties and she was in her seventies, simple arithmetic made them all about fifty and gave each of them fifteen years to go before retirement. It was an ingenious solution, but certainly not the one the accrediting board had in mind.

Somehow the reports were compiled, nevertheless, and handsomely bound in a fat volume, padded out with all the academic jargon Dr. Norden and I had tried to delete, and noteworthy chiefly for its unique system of random punctuation. As with so many things about Thomas, the best aspect of the report was its cover—neat, glossy, and very official. Copies were distributed to the faculty at a special meeting called to discuss the completed project, but when faculty members questioned some points of information in the report, Greeson counseled them at length that in a project so large it is unreasonable to expect perfection. Even if its errors were discounted, the report was already obsolete, for it was based on conditions of the previous year and disregarded many changes—some for the better, most for the worse—that had occurred in the interim. Within hours of the deadline, dozens of copies of the report were dispatched to the accreditation board, and the college waited anxiously for a response.

Completion of the self-study, however, was only one of many requirements for accreditation. In addition, the accrediting board of the regional Association of Colleges and Schools had established a number of "standards" that were supposed to be met by any college seeking accreditation. Whether a college successfully measured up to the standards or not was to be determined by the board's inspectors, specialists in various areas of instruction and administration selected from accredited colleges that were members of the regional association.

Standard One specified that each college should state in clear and concise prose a "purpose, not only worthy of higher education in general, but also appropriate for its specific educational role." [1] To formulate an official purpose is a simple task, and Thomas had met the challenge grandly.

> Thomas College is devoted to the attainment and propagation of knowledge, the search for truth, and the pursuit of wisdom, and the application of these principles, facts, and skills to the perpetuation of a Christian environment and climate productive of the proper maturation of the mind, body, and spirit of the developing individual. Thomas College stimulates the capacities of its students to reason, to acquire a respect for the values of culture, to compete intellectually, and the capacity for acquisition of high moral principles and social relations. Hence, Thomas College is a coeducational institution which offers liberal education, preprofessional programs, and professional education for teachers. Moreover, Thomas College endeavors to give all those who enter into this institution preparation for life.

This statement of purpose may not exactly be clear and

[1] *The College Blue Book 1969/70*, Vol. 8, ed. Max Russell (New York: CCM Information Corporation, n.d.), p. 245. Subsequent quotations from the Standards of the College Delegate Assembly of the Southern Association of Colleges and Schools are drawn from this volume, pp. 244–57.

concise, but it is, in its way, impressive. The accrediting board, however, expects a college not only to state a purpose but also to fulfill it. "All institutional programs," the board says, ". . . should be designed to achieve the stated purpose." But when an institution's purpose is as broad as Thomas's, how does one determine whether it is being fulfilled or not? How does an inspector who visits the Thomas campus for a few days tell whether the college is in fact preparing its students "for life"?

Secondly, the regional association is concerned with the organization and administration of colleges. The board states that "the administrative organization of an institution of higher learning should bring together its various resources and coordinate them effectively to accomplish its objectives. . . . The organizational structure and the administrative processes should be well defined and understood by the entire college community." To make the organizational structure clear to all members of the college, the board strongly recommends "formalized faculty manuals." Complying with this suggestion, President Greeson had obtained a foundation grant and had compiled a faculty guide containing a job description for everyone in the school from himself down to the lowliest file clerk. Yet in preparing a guide *for* the faculty—a term that at Thomas includes the file clerks— Greeson had fulfilled the letter but violated the spirit of the standard. The board assumes that "an effective pattern of organization will contribute to the development of the institution and to general morale. Opportunities for adequate communications through the institution are highly important." At Thomas, of course, despite the richly detailed faculty guide, there was no communication, and the general morale was abysmal.

Similarly, to comply with the terms of the board's third standard, Thomas had taken some stop-gap measures to improve the educational program. Since the board had instructed the school to formulate an admissions policy, Thomas drew up an appropriate statement. To be considered for admission to Thomas, a student was supposed to submit evidence of his high school graduation and his scores on the American College Test; but he could take the test after he enrolled at Thomas, and if he hadn't completed high school, he could obtain "special permission" to enter the college anyway. In other words, anyone who applied and paid the nonrefundable five-dollar application fee was admitted. To handle admissions and record keeping, the board called for an admissions officer or registrar. Thomas appointed one: a very pleasant young lady, a Thomas graduate with some secretarial training. The board advised that "responsibility for curriculum control and administration should be assigned to a committee of the faculty and administrative official." Consequently, Dean Butler hastily formed the impotent Committee on Standards and Instructional Programs. The board declared that "instruction should be related to the objectives of each course" and that the "process of instruction should be organized so that students have a clear idea of the aims and requirements of each course," so Thomas produced course outlines.

Whenever the board's standard could be met by the composition of a policy statement or the appointment of an inept official or powerless committee, Thomas complied. When meeting the board's standard involved real work or genuine reform, Thomas ignored the recommendations. Thus, it overlooked the board's requirement that "effectiveness of instruction should be under continuous study", and the prescription for follow-up studies and opinion polls of its former students. Although the board insisted that "the catalog and other published materials concerning institutional offerings should accurately and honestly reflect the academic resources of the institution," Thomas continued to distribute its glossy brochure replete with descriptions of nonexistent courses and programs. The board's assertions that "effective instruction depends largely upon the general environment in the institution" and that "an institution of higher education should endeavor to create a climate of intellectual curiosity and achievement among its students" made Thomas officials understandably uneasy but did not inspire them to positive action.

The accrediting board was also concerned with the college's financial resources, requiring that the school give evidence of stability and a diversity of sources of income. Stressing the importance of endowments to non-tax-supported institutions, the board affirmed that "an institution having available income from this source strengthens the base of stability." Thomas had an endowment, but its endowment earnings were only $20,500 in 1969 and $24,500 in 1970, providing less than half of 1 per cent of the school's income, hardly enough to strengthen its "base of stability" appreciably. Thomas reports that roughly one-fifth to one-quarter of its income derives from private gifts and grants, probably largely from educational foundations. All of the college's other apparent sources of income, however, exist mainly on paper; the monies reportedly received from student tuition and fees and the profits of the school cafeteria, store, and laundry actually come ultimately from the state and federal governments. Thus, although the Thomas budget may appear sound, it scarcely represents a diversity of sources of income. Receiving about three-quarters of its income either directly or indirectly from government, Thomas has become, in effect, a tax-supported institution; its "base of stability" is the Department of Health, Education, and Welfare.

Thomas's skill at apparently fulfilling the letter of the accreditation board's law is most evident in its policies regarding faculty. "Standard Five" of the accrediting board deals with the "selection, development, and retention of a competent faculty," a matter of "major importance." At Thomas, however, recruitment of faculty did not entail the "active and painstaking search" the board recommends but instead amounted to a kind of grab-bag procedure conducted almost exclusively by President Greeson. Thanks to HEW grants for visiting scholars and national teaching fellows and to educational-foundation grants for faculty travel, Thomas could produce evidence that it was encouraging "professional development by affording opportunities, such as, leaves of absence for study and research, research facilities, membership in professional organizations, attendance at professional meetings and workshops, and in-service training." Yet the college used the money at its disposal, not to encourage the faculty "to exercise initiative in identifying and meeting [their] own professional growth needs," but rather to bribe them into obedience.

The board also stated its position on the issue of faculty job security.

> The policies and procedures for the termination of appointments should be stated in writing and should be in accord with commonly accepted practices. Termination of non-tenure members of the teaching staff should be made only after adequate notice has been given. Termination of the appointments of those members of the staff with tenure should be made only for cause, and the individual should be fully protected with the proper safeguards.

To comply with that position, Greeson included in his faculty guide a lengthy statement on faculty tenure and the termination of employment, but the entire Thomas faculty was to learn, soon after the departure of the last accreditation inspectors, just how hollow the rhetoric of the Thomas tenure policy actually was. And like the tenure policy, the criteria for faculty evaluation and promotion in rank—criteria also recommended by the board—were well publicized but rarely adhered to.

The official policy of the college on the question of faculty organization was less clear-cut. The faculty did meet regularly, as the board advised, but only to listen to President Greeson's sermons. Since the board dictated only that "faculty membership should be clearly defined," Thomas may have been within its rights in defining janitors and secretaries as faculty members. The board also stated, however, that "the jurisdiction of the faculty in academic affairs should be clearly defined and should provide adequate scope for the exercise of faculty responsibility. The faculty should be concerned primarily with fundamental academic policies." The faculty at Thomas, of course, had no jurisdiction whatsoever; its jurisdiction thus was "clearly defined," but it hardly provided "adequate scope." Nevertheless, the faculty's rubber-stamp votes at Greeson's faculty meetings probably provided sufficient evidence to the inspectors that the faculty was exercising its "responsibility."

HEW grants for visiting scholars and national teaching fellows also helped the college to meet requirements for the academic preparation of the faculty. By using the money to hire Ph.D.'s and by counting administrators with Ed.D.'s along with the teachers, the college was able to demonstrate that close to the stipulated 30 per cent of its "faculty" held doctorates. The investigators would not have to know that those doctors, whose presence was assumed to upgrade the faculty, came and went under administration pressure like the tides, while the only faculty members who exerted any influence on the college at all were the good old retainers whose academic credentials in most cases seemed dubious.

Similarly, the faculty pay scale looked satisfactory on paper. The average pay for an associate or assistant professor in 1970 was $8,000 for nine months, a salary that is not exactly competitive with those of other institutions but still fairly respectable. And the maximum salary of $11,000 for one in these ranks is surely creditable. Those top salaries, which pull up the average, however, are paid by government grants; consequently, the minimum salaries paid for each rank probably measure much more accurately the "financial security" the college actually provides for most of its teachers. A full professor may earn as little as $4,800, an associate or assistant professor $2,600, an instructor $1,800. And although the accrediting board declares that a college should have "a program of benefits, including a sound retirement plan," Thomas had none. But the college, however, did not have to be overly concerned about faculty salaries and retirement benefits, for the accrediting board could be expected to look with charity upon a college that was prevented from fulfilling its admirable intentions only by a slight shortage of money that might be corrected after accreditation.

To meet the board's sixth standard, concerning library facilities and holdings, Thomas established a functionless faculty library committee, extended the library hours to the required minimum, and dusted the shelves. The librarian, a highly competent but overworked woman, tried to enlist professors to guide her crash program of acquisitions, a hurried and ill-considered buying spree to increase the library holdings to the prescribed minimum. Since so few professors had read widely in their fields, however, the faculty could offer little assistance in book selection, and the librarian purchased at random, seeking the greatest number of books for the least expenditure of money. After all, what seemed to matter to the board was the *number* of library books, not whether the books were current, significant, or related to courses at the college.

In the same haphazard fashion, Thomas attended to the board's standard regarding student personnel services: provisions for student activities, counseling, health services, student record keeping, and alumni records. Thomas established an office of student services, but it was not staffed by the "well-trained, qualified people" the board called for; it was manned by the same old dean of student affairs with a new sign on his office door. The "flexible, challenging, and current, . . . meaningful and helpful" orientation program the board prescribed became at Thomas the four-day indoctrination ordeal suffered by the freshmen. The "experienced counselors" who were supposed to help students with "academic, personal, and vocational problems" existed in name only. The required "current and accurate records of the addresses, occupations, and accomplishments of alumni" didn't exist at all.

The last of the board's requirements that pertained to Thomas called for "high standards of housekeeping, preventive maintenance, cleanliness, and care of grounds." Since the visiting inspectors would easily see how little attention Thomas paid to such trivialities, housekeeping became the college's major chore in the last weeks before inspection. The entire campus underwent a massive spring cleaning, its first in years. The effort began when President Greeson announced shortly before Christmas that the inspectors would be coming to visit the campus again. The board had assured Greeson that this visit would be final and decisive. From that point on, the college behaved like an adolescent boy primping for his first date, hitching up his socks with Scotch tape, slathering his pimples with acne cream, dousing his neck with Dad's after-shave, and frantically daubing his old brown shoes with shiny black polish.

In preparation for the crucial inspection, the college was visited time and again by three white consultants—a dean and two professors—from a neighboring private (and still largely segregated) university of very good reputation. They met with the members of each department to hear its progress report, with Dean Butler nervously leading the discussions so that only "progress" would be mentioned. They discovered that a faculty in-service training program, required by the board, had not been established and persuaded

Butler to hold a faculty meeting to discuss what such a
program should include. The emphasis at the meeting on
the quality of teaching made the faculty shift its defense.
Almost to a man, they argued that the quality of teaching in
their department was excellent and would be perfect if only
they could get the supplies they needed. Grievances were
listed, and the replies from other faculty members were instructive. The Spanish department needed tape recorders;
the speech department had a surplus. The French department wanted some typewriters; the typing teacher was over-
supplied. The math department could use adding machines;
the business department had many in storage. Nothing could
have made it clearer that faculty members never discussed
pedagogic matters with their colleagues.

During the meeting, a number of students were ushered
in to express their grievances to the consulting team. Seated
in the front of the room with all their teachers looking on
and Dean Butler presiding, they were asked to speak freely.
Not surprisingly, most of them pronounced the college an
ideal institution and expressed gratitude for the opportunity
it offered them. Only one young man spoke against the ruth-
less abridgment of students' rights and the miserable level
of instruction, but his comments were later explained away
by the dean as those of a professional griper and troublemaker. (Several weeks later, when the inspection team had
come and gone, the "troublemaker" was permanently expelled for fighting. His expulsion might have been a coincidence, but his adversary in the fight, who had started it,
went unpunished.)

The total absence of communication and cooperation
among students, faculty, and administration was too obvious
at that meeting to escape the notice of the consultants. If
the atmosphere of the campus, the symptom of its inner rot,
were seen by the accreditation team, the college would be
lost; for the board professed to be concerned primarily with

the vitality of the total institution. "Meeting each standard is not all that is required for accreditation by and membership in the . . . Association," the board warned.

> Assuredly, the Commission is interested in qualifications of faculty, the state of academic freedom, library size, and numerous other educational factors in an institutional operation. It is finally concerned, however, with the totality of the effort, and the atmosphere in which it is carried on. The assessment of this totality overrides smaller considerations as the decision is approached whether or not to confer or to retain membership.

And so the consultants, seeing that it was too late to change the substance of the college, concentrated on altering its appearance. They called committee meetings, staff meetings, department meetings, school meetings, faculty meetings, student meetings—all for the purpose of teaching us our manners. Time and again, they stressed the importance of a "positive attitude," which meant telling the inspectors about the college's good points and passing over our "personal grievances." If the college could successfully conceal its "atmosphere" from the inspectors while displaying paper proof of having met the standards, Thomas just might slip past the gates. For the board also assured applying schools that "no institution asking for membership will be refused if it demonstrates its acceptability under the standards of the Commission."

Almost everyone in the college "community" was more than willing to set aside his grievances, temporarily at least, for almost everyone had a vested interest in the success of the college. If the school failed in its bid for accreditation, it probably would be forced to close. Teachers would lose their jobs at a time when, because of the general economic squeeze, it was most difficult to find new ones. They faced the possibility of unemployment or of uprooting themselves and their families from congenial soil to find new jobs elsewhere. And although they weren't paid very well at Thomas, they would be unlikely to find other jobs that demanded so little responsibility and effort. For the administrators the prospects were even grimmer. The failure of the college meant personal failure for Greeson and Butler. Having publicly demonstrated their administrative ineptitude, they would not be entrusted with such high office again. At best, Greeson might find a petty deanship at another school like Thomas. Butler would probably have to return to teaching, starting his career all over again from the bottom.

The students, too, had an interest in Thomas's accreditation. Although most of them only vaguely understood the concept of accreditation, they had been told that it would distinguish their college as a "good" one. Presumably, accreditation would enhance the value of their diplomas and make them eligible for better jobs. Many students had enrolled at Thomas thinking that it already was accredited, a sound assumption since the college catalogue fails to mention that accreditation has been withdrawn. Such students, although angered by this deception, were now compelled to cooperate with the administration to gain the endorsement they had thought the school already possessed. None of the students realized how close the college was to going under, and consequently most of them received the attention of consultants and inspectors as a high honor; but having been told so often and so strenuously how to behave and what to say, they grew to feel that they themselves were on trial. Like the teachers and administrators, they, too, would behave. Under the firm tutelage of the distinguished consultants, whose own incentive was the $100-per-day consulting fee Thomas paid out of an HEW grant, everyone at Thomas would join—briefly, at least—into one big happy family.

Along with the indoctrination sessions training us in the behavior appropriate to a happy family went a flurry of last minute busywork. Professors hastily distributed course outlines and reading lists and lectured their students on the objectives of their courses so that students, if asked by an inspector, could explain what their course work was about and could produce the documentary evidence. Committee chairmen improvised minutes of meetings that had never been held and filed them in the president's office. The vice-president pored over his account books while the librarian pulled her most archaic volumes off the shelves and hid them in the basement.

President Greeson cloaked his taut nerves in a guise of studied seriousness, pacing in his black silk suit from one meeting to the next, sternly lecturing and firmly encouraging his underlings, transmitting the grave weight of the impending inspection and the somber mood that he always carried about him like an enveloping fog. Butler wore his nerves closer to the surface. With his shirtsleeves rolled and his loosened tie askew, he chugged about the campus, shouting orders he had given half a dozen times before, reducing secretaries to frustrated tears, stabbing at his sweating face with a soiled handkerchief, sometimes collapsing into his padded swivel chair to stare abstractedly at the new carpet on his office floor, his framed diplomas on the wall.

Meanwhile, the maintenance department worked overtime to give the campus a face lifting. While students cleared the campus of trash, the groundskeepers mowed and raked and weeded. For the first time, they planted flowers and shrubbery and painted neat white lines around the faculty parking spaces. Large rooms in which meetings might be held were given a fresh coat of green paint. The interior of the administration building and the decaying white columns on the library façade were painted for the first time in years. The students, too, were given cans of paint and coerced into redecorating their rooms under the watchful eyes of their house matrons. New desks were rolled into the faculty office building, while professors feverishly stuffed their files with papers. The faculty men's room was fitted out with paper towels and toilet paper, and when it was discovered that there would be a woman on the inspection team, the faculty ladies' room was similarly equipped. On the last day, while the students heard President Greeson and his wife lecture on good grooming, the janitors painted the flimsy, water-stained ceiling in the main classroom building, and, by the grace of God, the rain did not come pouring through again until the inspection team had concluded its visit. When the preparations were complete, when everything had been checked and checked again, the janitors hoisted over the immaculate campus a brand-new American flag.

The twelve-man inspection team was to be on the campus for a week, and the administrators, as hosts, had made careful provision for every moment of the visit, precluding the possibility of a chance encounter with some disgruntled professor or student. Each member of the team was provided with a guide, a hand-picked member of the administration or business staff, who clung to him like a shadow, leading him into conversations with professors and students who could be trusted to say the right things. Dean Butler himself accompanied inspectors to department meetings, and as a double precaution, he "forgot" to invite recalcitrant professors, like Dr. Norden and me, to the meetings. In midafternoon the inspectors were shepherded from the campus for cocktails and dinner at an administrator's home, where they chatted with a few carefully chosen faculty members each evening. Late in their visit, the inspectors, perhaps suspecting that they were not being given the whole picture, asked to meet privately with individual students. President Greeson, only a little uneasy, complied and sent them his first string of student leaders, that distinguished group of Toms and Judases who evoked in their fellow students a mixture of envy and hatred.

At the end of the week, the inspectors departed to make their reports to the accrediting board. President Greeson was optimistic, for his plans seemed to have worked exceedingly well. During the visit, neither Dr. Norden nor I had been able to speak to a single inspector, and I had not even seen one from a distance. Undoubtedly, we were pointed out to them, for as young Ph.D.'s recently added to the faculty, we had to be called to the attention of the accreditors, but we could not be allowed to speak with them because Greeson could not control what we might say. In fact, the only clue I had that the inspectors were on campus was that the food in the cafeteria was suddenly much better and more plentiful.

The inspection was over and there would not be another one. Several months later the regional association would meet to reach its decision, but until then the college would be free of consultants and inspectors. And if the board accredited the college, as the administrators thought it would, it would send no more inspectors for at least ten years. If the board decided against accreditation, the college probably would be forced to close in a year or two. In any case, the board would base its decision on the evidence already gathered; from now on, Greeson was free to do as he pleased.

Thus, within a week of the inspection team's visit, the college returned to normal. The weeds grew up and the flowers withered; the rain seeped through the roofs and the new paint began to peel. The professors got their old desks back, and the toilet paper ran out in the lavatories. Greeson, his old affability gone, had begun his austerity program to make up for the expenses of refurbishing the campus. He set the cafeteria back to red beans and sweet potatoes. He let it be known that the English department and the School of Arts and Letters would not get new chairmen as promised but that the devoted, and inexpensive, Dr. Harder would continue to serve. And he began to fire from the faculty all the Ph.D.'s—his most expensive professors—and the old-timers whom he knew he could later buy back cheaper. Less than a week after the inspectors left, Greeson and Butler had decimated the English faculty and totally wiped out the French and Spanish departments and the entire School of Science. The salaries of those who had already committed themselves to teach in summer school were drastically cut, and unstaffed summer-school programs were simply dropped altogether. Outspoken students were expelled without appeal. Secretaries who knew too well how to type up phony reports—the president's, the dean's, the vice-president's—suddenly disappeared. The purge was swift, sudden, and complete. Greeson knew his slaves well. They received the lash with great lamentation, but no active protest.

The whole charade of consultants, recommendations, self-studies, reports, and inspections was over. But why, I wondered, had so many people spent so many years in obvious self-deception? The very first consultants could have reported the inescapable truth that the college was hopeless and should be closed. Instead they had filed endless recommendations. The distinguished preinspection consultants could have told the board the same thing, although doing so would have cost them their handsome consulting fees. Instead they had participated in the farce and, although sent out by the accrediting board, had arranged the means of deceiving the board's inspectors. The expenditure of time and money on the part of everyone involved had been profligate and meaningless. The key to the situation, as to so many paradoxes of American society, was racism.

At the first preinspection faculty meeting, one of the eminent white university professors on the consulting team had told us that, "to be perfectly frank," one of the strongest points the college had in its favor was "the great desire of so many educators, businessmen, and statesmen today in our state, and indeed all across our region, to see 'you people' improve your schools." What he meant, of course, was that if the poor black colleges were not kept open, blacks would go in increasing numbers to the cheaper and better state colleges and universities or out into the labor market to compete with white students and laborers. Unless they could be kept in their own schools as long as possible, the blacks would take white men's jobs and perhaps their daughters as well. Closing the poor black colleges was the first step toward intermarriage, Communism, and general chaos.

It is easy to make fun of the wild fears of racists, but some of these fears are well-grounded. Had Thomas and schools like it closed their doors, many of their black students probably would have gone to better colleges and universities, both black and integrated, to encounter new ideas and experiences. They might have met for the first time ideas that helped them to understand their own oppressed lives and white people of their own age who treated them as fellow human beings. Other students, unable to gain admission to college, would have entered the labor market and, unable to get decent jobs for honest wages, might have become frustrated, angry, even militant. With blacks all across the country boiling with unrest, it had become more difficult and more important than ever for the white man to keep the lid shut tight.

In holding down the lid, colleges like Thomas provide indispensable muscle. Run by "colored" bourgeois who take their cut and know their place, the colleges train another generation of young blacks to know theirs. Greeson and his like, by constantly browbeating and humiliating their students, by transforming them into psychological Sambos, were doing the white man's work for him. As a local white man explained to me, "There ain't nobody better at keepin' a nigger in his place than a nigger in a better one." For just that reason, Simon L. Greeson, the master, and Thomas College, the updated version of the old plantation, had become indispensable to the white world, and white men and black men alike gladly made fools of themselves to preserve the system that had been so painstakingly built over generations. If the accreditation procedure was insane, it was no more so than the society that had produced it.

8

Toward Emancipation

For one year I was part of the establishment of the institution described in these pages, and as such I was compelled to evaluate my own position. Although I was very much involved with my students and would like to have stuck by them, my analysis of the institution led me inevitably to the conclusion that Thomas College and schools like it should be closed. I have no quarrel with the many good black colleges. Schools like Thomas, however, not only fail to educate their students but also go a long way toward perpetuating the stereotypes on which a racist society thrives. For this very reason, it is clearly in the interest of that racist society to keep such schools in business.

To argue that colleges like Thomas should be put out of business is a very serious matter. After all, the black colleges, including Thomas, have made an enormous contribution to American society over the years, a contribution too seldom acknowledged. Since white America largely refused the responsibility of providing higher education for black citizens, the black colleges have educated most of the black college students in this country. Within less than a century, teachers trained by black colleges spread literacy among the black population. In 1860, 95 per cent of American blacks were illiterate; by 1960, black illiteracy had almost entirely disappeared. This astonishing accomplishment can be attributed almost exclusively to the black colleges. These schools are also largely responsible for the development of the black middle class, from which has emerged an articulate black leadership. Dr. Martin Luther King, Jr., Whitney Young, Jr., Stokely Carmichael, and many other prominent Americans graduated from black colleges. According to a recent estimate, black colleges "probably account for four-fifths or more of all [American] black college graduates alive today." [1] Even today black colleges still educate more than half of all black college students in the United States.[2] Black colleges also have been the caretakers of the Afro-American heritage in this country, preserving through the most bitter days at least the traces of a distinctly black culture. In view of their extraordinary accomplishments, one cannot speak lightly of closing even a handful of these colleges.

But much more than historical accomplishment is at stake. If Thomas and similar very small, poor-quality black colleges closed their doors tomorrow, what would become of their students? Many of them are good enough scholars to be admitted to the better black colleges or to predominantly white colleges, but most are unaware of these alternatives and of the financial aid potentially available to them. Such students undoubtedly receive very little counseling in their high schools. They learn of colleges from the colleges themselves, and the poor-quality black schools seem to recruit most intensively. In recent years, the poor-quality colleges have expanded more rapidly than the good ones; in fact, the good

[1] Thomas F. Pettigrew, "The Black Colleges," *Intellectual Digest* (March, 1972), p. 75.

[2] Earl J. McGrath, *The Predominantly Negro Colleges and Universities in Transition* (New York: Columbia University, Teachers College Bureau of Publications, 1965), p. 158.

black colleges have shown the smallest increases in enrollments. Between 1962 and 1965 the poor black colleges in the
Deep South increased their enrollments almost 50 per cent,[3]
and, as more and more federal aid pours into these schools
and into student loan programs, the trend will probably continue. A recent study indicates that over a third of the "more
able" Southern black college entrants enroll in substandard
schools. Even more disturbing is the finding that about half
of the more able Southern black high school graduates don't
enter college at all.[4]

It seems clear that the better black colleges must intensify
their recruitment efforts and that the federal government
must support these schools in their recruitment and ex-
pansion plans. Similarly, largely white colleges that are committed to equal opportunity must seek out able black high
school graduates.

Assuring a good higher education for able black students
would seem to be largely a matter of finding them, providing
counseling, and offering financial aid. But what is to become
of the not-so-able student, the typical Thomas undergraduate, who is deprived of a fair start by poverty and a second-
rate lower-school system? One cannot simply shut down
schools like Thomas without providing for the education of
most of their students.

Many educators, black and white, are aware of this
dilemma and have offered several alternative suggestions.
A. J. Jaffe and his colleagues, who studied black higher education in the sixties, suggest that federal funds currently

[3] A. J. Jaffe, Walter Adams, and Sandra G. Meyers, *Negro Higher Education in the 1960's* (New York: Praeger, 1968), p. 127. Jaffe and his colleagues
evaluated black colleges according to a set of standard educational criteria
such as might be used by any accrediting agency. Categorizing the colleges as
"good," "fair," and "poor," they studied the development of each of these
groups, noting the trend I have cited. For purposes of this discussion I have
accepted their categories; their book may be consulted for an explication of
their criteria and methodology.

[4] *Ibid.*, p. 133.

being given to poor and fair black colleges should be used instead to establish a network of integrated public two-year colleges throughout the South. These junior colleges would be low-cost commuter schools offering curricula designed to meet the employment needs of the area and to provide easy transfer to four-year state colleges for those desiring additional study.

My own experience makes me skeptical of this proposal. Many Thomas students could easily have commuted from their homes to existing public junior colleges, but they chose the more expensive course of taking up residence at Thomas. When asked why, they claimed that athletes were the only black students admitted to the junior colleges. Whether that claim is true or not, it reflects their profound feeling that they could not attend the predominantly white schools, or that they could do so only at the cost of incurring great hostility. The preference that Thomas students have shown for a black college, however bad, over a predominantly white one must not be ignored.

Nor should it be forgotten that black colleges were established in the first place because the white society simply would not provide higher education for blacks. Contrary to the popular notion that racism is gradually disappearing, the history of race relations in America is charted on an erratic graph of good periods and bad. The unpleasant fact is that racism persists as a national disease and may erupt in its most virulent forms at any moment. Therefore, it seems to me idle to suppose that giving a large share of the responsibility for black education over to white-dominated public colleges, which historically have been criminally irresponsible, will solve the problem.

Earl J. McGrath, on the other hand, believes that "it would be patent foolishness to close existing colleges while establishing new institutions." [5] He calls instead for massive

[5] McGrath, *op. cit.*, p. 9.

federal support for *all* black colleges, however small and undistinguished. That Thomas has received so much money and shown so little improvement, however, might indicate that the amount of aid is less important than the way it is used. But how money is used, like all matters of policy at Thomas, is decided by the president, and there is no sign that increasing the amount of money given to him will improve the quality of his administration.

Unfortunately, the Thomas pattern of presidential domination is common among black colleges. This traditional patriarchal administrative structure—what I call the plantation structure—probably developed from necessity. For decades, the black colleges occupied a very precarious position; they were marginal institutions in a hostile white society. Indeed, some still are. Surely one of the chief duties of the president must have been to protect the existence of his college and his students. He became, in a very real sense, the patriarch. For at least the past thirty years, however, educators have observed that this patriarchal structure not only is obsolete but has become the biggest obstacle to significant improvement in black higher education. McGrath himself notes the problem, citing the summary of the 1942 *National Survey of the Higher Education of Negroes:* "The organization [of black colleges] is authoritarian, and important decisions relative to academic affairs are made by the administrative officers." [6] Similarly, Tilden J. LeMelle and Wilbert J. LeMelle, prominent black educators familiar with the traditional pattern, call for an end to "presidentialism":

"Presidentialism," or the tendency to relegate arbitrary and absolute decision-making power to the office of the president, is no longer defensible or possible in the black colleges. . . . The principal administrative need in the black colleges is for

[6] Ambrose Caliver, *National Survey of the Higher Education of Negroes: A Summary* (Washington: U.S. Office of Education, 1943), p. 27; quoted in McGrath, *op. cit.,* p. 123.

a new alignment of decision-making power. Decentralization of presidential power to rightful levels of decision-making in the college structure is a priority requirement for progressive development. A new pattern of power-sharing is the only remedy that will curb authoritarian excess and replace the present dysfunctional bureaucracy with effective management systems.[7]

Nevertheless, despite attacks by the LeMelle brothers and other educators, the plantation structure persists at Thomas. So long as that is the case, money—even massive infusions of it—will not help significantly. The best one can hope for under the plantation system is an intelligent, courageous, creative master. Unfortunately, the number of intelligent, courageous, creative college presidents of any color has never been overwhelming.

The LeMelle brothers, however, pass beyond the usual criticism that poor black colleges provide substandard education. The real failure of black colleges, they maintain, lies in their inability to stimulate black consciousness, to foster black identity.

The prime responsibility for this failure to provide the answer to the search for complete liberation of the black personality during the past hundred years must be assumed by the traditional Negro college because it alone has had the capacity and opportunity to provide the answer. The dilemma of being black in the United States, together with the accompanying compulsive ambivalence and insecurity derived from horribly twisted self-attitudes, could be successfully challenged and dispelled only through the conscious nurturing of antithetical attitudes and values representing a positive and balanced image of the black man and his blackness. To construct, develop, and steadfastly assert the redeeming image of the free black man was obviously an intellectual undertaking requiring the highest skill and commitment of those responsible for imparting a philosophy and a sense of values in the educational

[7] Tilden J. LeMelle and Wilbert J. LeMelle, *The Black College: A Strategy for Achieving Relevancy* (New York: Praeger, 1969), p. 85.

process. Regrettably, black scholars failed to concern themselves with the self-alienation of black students. Through the
years scholars at the traditional Negro colleges have done
irreparable harm by providing only a sterile conformist educational experience for the best of black American youth.
Tragically, such education served more to confirm the black
dilemma than to destroy it. Black higher education must re-
discover its prime purpose—to free the mind and spirit of
black youth.[8]

To counter this failure, the LeMelle brothers suggest a
new "strategy for relevance," a new black consciousness in
every aspect of black higher education that would "establish
black as a legitimate point of reference in U.S. society."

> As it stands now, in its racial context the only legitimate point
> of reference in the U.S. is white—and that is the essence of
> racism. It is only through establishing black as another legiti-
> mate point of reference that the black American can attain
> first-class citizenship and the curse of racism can be neu-
> tralized.[9]

The program proposed by the LeMelle brothers to transform the traditional Negro college into a truly black college,
producing students who are not only well educated but
secure in their own identity, seems to me an ideal well
worth seeking by black and white alike. But how? Changing
the philosophy of an established institution is infinitely more
difficult than reforming a few procedures. As the LeMelles
point out, there is "fierce resistance" from the top of the
patriarchal structure to "widening the decision-making
process." [10] Moreover, the people who are most likely to
initiate change, the young faculty members, are precisely
those who have been most repressed by autocratic admini-
strations.

In the traditional Negro college young faculty have been par-

[8] *Ibid.,* p. 30.
[9] *Ibid.,* pp. 132–33.
[10] *Ibid.,* p. 86.

ticularly affected by administrative rigor and intolerance on the question of absolute conformity and imitation of the usually irrelevant "mainstream" educational principles, practices, and objectives. Commonly, not only have young faculty been discouraged from experimenting with new modes of attacking the complex learning problems of their students, but in many cases they have been specifically prohibited from creatively diverting from the typical "educationally sound" practices.[11]

Such was certainly the case at Thomas. There were, in fact, two or three black faculty members there who might have reshaped the college closer to the LeMelles' proposal had any of them been named president. But they would have been the last to be nominated to administrative posts; it was all they could do to forestall outright dismissal. As a matter of fact, Thomas once had a president who tried to reshape the college—but the board of trustees pressed him to resign. Nevertheless, the fact that black educators advocate radical change is heartening.

In the meantime, until black colleges develop a true black consciousness, what is to be done for the not-so-able Thomas student? I would suggest that HEW divert funds from the poor black colleges to the good ones, encouraging the latter to expand. At present none of the black colleges are very large. Only 10 per cent of students in black colleges are enrolled in the two schools with more than 5,000 students, while 58 per cent of the other American college students attend schools of at least this size, with many enrolled in much larger institutions. On the other hand, 35 per cent of black college students are in institutions of fewer than 1,000 students, but less than 12 per cent of other students attend such small schools.[12] Small colleges, of course, usually have more limited programs, less specialized facilities, and heavier teaching loads; and they are less economical to operate.

[11] *Ibid.*, pp. 27–28.
[12] McGrath, *op. cit.*, p. 22.

With adequate funding, the good black colleges could expand and might be persuaded to admit those not-so-able students who don't meet regular admission standards, providing them with intensive compensatory work. Programs in New York and elsewhere indicate that even students who have been severely deprived in elementary and high school respond well to intelligent and sympathetic help. At the present time, I teach at an urban college in the North in a compensatory writing program designed to fill the needs of students who have been admitted without qualifying under the regular admissions standards. Those of us who work in the program commonly see remarkable improvement in the students' ability to express themselves clearly in written standard English; and improvement in English usually produces improvement in other subjects as well, for the traditional term papers and essay exams of college courses often measure not the student's knowledge of history or psychology or philosophy but his ability to convey that knowledge in standard English prose. In fact, some ghetto students who entered the college under a special program for educationally deprived youngsters a few years ago are already working on their graduate degrees. We don't possess any magic formula for compensatory education, but we do have a large, deeply dedicated staff of skillful people engaging in constant experimentation, research, and dialogue, and sharing a commitment to educational change.

The students at Thomas seem not very different from black students in this Northern program; in fact, many of their problems are similar. None of them are the "dummies" they are assumed to be at Thomas. The Southern black student from a cropper's shanty in the Delta, like his cousin from Harlem or Bedford-Stuyvesant, usually has not *failed* to learn. More often than not, he has never been taught—but he can be.

Compensatory programs could be developed at many other

colleges, both black and integrated, with federal financial assistance. Among black colleges, it is the good ones, with a long tradition of quality education, that would seem best equipped to transform educationally deprived students into successful ones. Surely, it is in the public interest that federal agencies provide them the funds for doing so. One can only speculate on the real changes that might have occurred in students' lives had the federal millions pumped into Thomas and schools like it in recent years been used instead to support compensatory programs at universities such as Atlanta, Howard, Fisk, Southern, or any of a dozen other black colleges, and at integrated urban colleges committed to rescuing students from city ghettos.

Such programs constitute only one of several alternatives to the poor black colleges. Decisions must properly rest with black educators, but my experience at Thomas has convinced me that some alternative must be chosen as quickly as possible. What is needed among educators, black and white, is commitment to change, for as long as higher education remains elitist it will educate only those who probably could educate themselves, and it will relegate the masses to schools like Thomas. Colleges, black and white, have long upheld the values of the society; they could help to change the society. They could begin by retrieving those who have been left standing at the starting gate. They could begin by making the Thomas colleges of this country as unnecessary as they are obsolete.

But there is another objection to closing black colleges like Thomas, an objection suggested by the LeMelle brothers' concern for black consciousness. Proponents, both black and white, of black colleges argue that the all-black college may be the answer to the persistent problem of black identity. In an all-black environment, they contend, black people can be free at last from the influence of Mr. Charlie; free from the need to defend against, or even to consider, the white point of view; free to relate to others and to themselves as black people. Having gained assurance of their own identity, graduates of black colleges will be better prepared to deal with the larger, largely white society.

I am in sympathy with this position. Indeed, if I were a black student I would choose to attend a black college for precisely this reason. I have found that, in consciousness-raising groups of the women's liberation movement, women are able to come to terms with each other and with themselves on new levels of openness and honesty. They need not stop to explain to men experiences and feelings that they, by virtue of being female, share and understand implicitly. Nor must they justify feelings that men might not approve, but that are nonetheless common. The single-sex group is arbitrary and artificial, yet in this setting I have seen more than one woman unfurl and become herself. Just so, the black college is arbitrary and artificial with reference to the larger society, but within its confines black identity, individual identity, may flourish.

This argument, however, presupposes that the women's group or the black college will be a good one. Such is not always the case. One women's group to which I belonged briefly, for example, consisted of harried housewives; they were all mothers of small children, wives of very ambitious and dominant men, and—worst of all—educated women. Their discussions centered on the logistics of their positions. ("How can I get the lunch dishes done and the baby to bed and still have time to read before starting dinner?" Answer: Use paper plates at lunch.) For such women, who have to obtain their husbands' permission to attend "group," paper plates constitute a major technological advance toward what they call liberation. They never question their assigned roles as domestic servants; they are concerned only with "learning to cope."

Similarly, the black college of which I write suppresses

questions about the traditional culturally assigned roles of black people in this society. It is concerned, rather, with teaching its students to adapt. Historically, of course, this attitude has been justified; adaptation has been a technique for survival in a racist land. More recently, however, militant black leaders have demonstrated that servile acceptance of white domination is no longer "where it's at." Nevertheless, servile acceptance is the doctrine Thomas continues to teach.

Many educators would argue that the issue of black identity transcends the question of quality education. A black student, they contend, has more to gain from a mediocre course in black poetry than from a superb course in Milton. But what is to be said in defense of a black college that still *requires* a course in Milton and offers none in black poetry? Where administrators and faculty assume that black people *are* inferior, how are students to learn otherwise? Where students are taught to be slaves, how are they to find themselves as people? Many Thomas students have acquired that most awesome quality of black Americans—the capacity to endure. But people who have been taught to kneel, although they may learn to walk, may find their legs, and their lives, permanently bent.

In short, if I were a black student, I would go to a black college; but I would not go to Thomas. Nor could I remain a teacher at Thomas, viewing it as I did as a school for servility. Some other faculty members who recognized the defects of the school felt that they should remain to "help the students." But I was never able to estimate my own impact so highly; and the over-all effect of the college upon the students was, as I saw it, disastrous. Thus, after one year, although I was offered another teaching contract, I left Thomas College. Many of my students viewed my departure as an act of betrayal, but I have not forgotten them.

Postscript

Nine months after the accrediting board's final inspection visit, the Southern Association of Colleges and Schools met and voted to grant accreditation and full membership to Thomas College. The association presented the college with an engraved certificate of accreditation.

Four months later, the Division of College Support, Bureau of Higher Education, Office of Education, Department of Health, Education, and Welfare, formally notified the Congress of the United States that it had awarded Thomas College a Title III grant of $100,000 annually for the next three years.